THE EMOTIONALLY INTELLIGENT TEAM

THE EMOTIONALLY INTELLIGENT TEAM

Understanding and Developing the Behaviors of Success

Marcia Hughes

James Bradford Terrell

JOSSEY-BASS
A Wiley Imprint
www.josseybass.com

Published by Jossey-Bass
A Wiley Imprint
989 Market Street, San Francisco, CA 94103—www.josseybass.com

Wiley Bicentennial logo: Richard J. Pacifico

Readers should be aware that Internet Web sites offered as citations and/or sources for further information may have changed or disappeared between the time this was written and when it is read.

Limit of Liability/Disclaimer of Warranty: While the publisher and author have used their best efforts in preparing this book, they make no representations or warranties with respect to the accuracy or completeness of the contents of this book and specifically disclaim any implied warranties of merchantability or fitness for a particular purpose. No warranty may be created or extended by sales representatives or written sales materials. The advice and strategies contained herein may not be suitable for your situation. You should consult with a professional where appropriate. Neither the publisher nor author shall be liable for any loss of profit or any other commercial damages, including but not limited to special, incidental, consequential, or other damages.

Jossey-Bass books and products are available through most bookstores. To contact Jossey-Bass directly, call our Customer Care Department within the United States at (800) 956-7739, outside the United States at (317) 572-3986, or via fax at (317) 572-4002.

Jossey-Bass also publishes its books in a variety of electronic formats. Some content that appears in print may not be available in electronic books.

Library of Congress Cataloging-in-Publication Data
Hughes, Marcia M.
  The emotionally intelligent team: understanding and developing the behaviors of success/Marcia Hughes, James Bradford Terrell. — 1st ed.
    p. cm.
  Includes bibliographical references and index.
  ISBN-13: 978-0-7879-8834-0 (cloth)
1. Teams in the workplace.   2. Emotional intelligence.   3. Interpersonal communication.
4. Organizational behavior. I. Terrell, James Bradford, 1951- II. Title.
  HD66.H84 2007
  658.3'128—dc22
                                                                                    2007011631

Printed in the United States of America
FIRST EDITION
HB Printing   10 9 8 7 6 5 4 3 2 1

CONTENTS

THE EMOTIONALLY INTELLIGENT TEAM

We dedicate this book to the teams and individual team members throughout the world whose commitment to their work and the work of their organizations help to create sustainable ways to live together on this planet, ways that reduce human suffering and expand our care for the precious diversity of life. We fervently advocate for the application of all tools and methods that can advance humanity's development of emotional and social intelligence.

INTRODUCTION

Everyone has inside of him a piece of good news.
The good news is that you don't know how great
you can be! How much you can love! What you can
accomplish! And what your potential is!
ANNE FRANK

Forget about the "flavor of the month" management strategy fraught with consultants and catchy programs: this isn't that book. This is about how to thrive in this nutty world and nuttier business environment by intentionally evolving, albeit quickly, because you can't even afford to wait a year, let alone a couple of hundred millennia. Your organization is on the edge of obsolescence if it's not evolving its emotional and social intelligence (ESI). You've heard the bottom line before: IQ is important, but emotional intelligence is the true brain trust of the organization. Using emotional intelligence effectively is the next evolution of human enterprise.

The world has changed. Once we thought it was flat. It wasn't. Once we thought it was run by monolithic factories and assembly lines built to last. It's not. Once we thought that an M.B.A. and wireless technology would secure the future. They won't. Reams of research all point to a single golden ticket. The passport to sustained viability is emotional intelligence.

There is great news for teams. The fields of neurology and organizational development are advancing so quickly that a body of evidence has emerged that demonstrates which emotionally and socially intelligent behaviors have a direct correlation with organizational success. We're talking about measurable success, not simply an improvement on the "feel-good meter." There are practical steps to take as an individual, a team member, and a leader that yield tangible results such as improved productivity, higher profits, lower turnover, fewer errors, greater innovation, and better efficiency—the Holy Grail of successful organizations. Our focus on team emotional and social intelligence is truly a practical opportunity to evolve and prosper.

The purpose of this book is to clarify the systematic process that will enable you to reduce the unproductive conflict, uncertainty, and delays all teams encounter. It will help teams of all shapes and sizes respond more resiliently to the continuous onslaught of change they must tame and transform into successful projects and productive results.

Every team—whether it's a permanent work team, a committee, a project team, or a family—needs better ESI. If you are involved in a team, that team has deep and significant emotional interactions, guaranteed. Furthermore, by virtue of being on a team, you are in a social environment. Because these emotional and social implications for your team are enormous, it is imperative that you care, if you care to succeed. *The Emotionally Intelligent Team* applies to all kinds of teams—at work, at play, at church, on the diamond, on the gridiron, or anywhere else. Because so much research and attention is focused on teams in the workplace, we drew most of our examples from there. Our research and examples span a wide spectrum of team types, from industry to government to nonprofits. You'll encounter a rich diversity of executive teams, departmental teams, IT teams, construction teams, nonprofit boards, and many more. The list is long and colorful. The principles that affect team dynamics are true, regardless of whether it is an interdisciplinary medical team, a group of high school cheerleaders, or contenders for the Super Bowl. Sports teams epitomize the profound role that emotions have in the workplace—it's the same as on the field. Nervous energy, jubilation, panic, anxiety as the momentum shifts, utter despair, supreme joy. How teams manage the extreme range of emotions that are packed into a game often determines the outcome.

One of the beauties of sports is the unabashed role and importance accorded to emotional intelligence. Its presence is considered a huge competitive advantage, while its absence is often criticized as the hallmark of an undisciplined team. Corporations and nonprofits would do well to recognize the same.

KEY CONCEPTS

> *The real act of discovery consists not in finding new lands but in seeing with new eyes.*
> MARCEL PROUST

Emotional and social intelligence is all about seeing with new eyes, hearing with new ears, and acting with new awareness and sensitivity. The key concepts that frame this book are the following:

- **Emotional and Social Intelligence (ESI).** Because it is impossible for a group of people to interact and not have social implications, we use the concept of emotional and social intelligence to help teams understand and master the behaviors of success. We have developed one of the first tools designed for determining team ESI, not just individual ESI. The Collaborative Growth Team Emotional and Social Intelligence Survey (TESI™) is a self-assessment tool used to help team members recognize and develop specific skills for success. (The survey will be published in 2008; you can contact us if you'd like more information.)
- **Collaborative Intelligence.** Collaboration is a composite skill that emerges from the masterful use of your ESI skills. The members of a football team collaborate when they huddle and agree that they will each do their part to execute a particular play. In the middle of the play, except in the face of an unexpected opportunity, the fullback won't decide to change the play because he'd prefer to run the ball rather than block! Team loyalty is unquestioned. When your team collaborates, you take time to explore alternative answers and find a solution that integrates the wisdom of the team. It takes more time up front, because you invest in listening to one another, to thinking things through, and to coordinating the execution of your response with genuine respect for one another. Collaboration pays off big time as you and your team progress.

Your self-discipline and collective intuition will make the future much easier to navigate because teams that coordinate their ESI skills naturally act with collaborative intelligence.

This set of coordinated competencies is the birthplace of synergy. Teams tap into their shared memory and individual capacities to maximize their knowledge, problem-solving capabilities, and resilience. They respond with agility to the fluctuating emotional and social contexts of the team and the organizational dynamics. The correct blend of ESI skills is the rocket fuel that propels your team to achieve its full collaborative capacity.

- **Emotional Literacy for Your Team.** Team smarts are the powerful result of learning to read. Read between the lines, read the writing on the wall, read people's lips! Team smarts call for:

    Reading one another to understand how you feel and why, to determine the most effective response given the situation.
    Reading the group as a whole to determine what is needed to keep your team highly energized and effective.
    Reading the environment and accurately discerning and responding to the organization and leadership dynamics, politics, and shifting winds.

THE GEOGRAPHY OF THE EMOTIONALLY INTELLIGENT TEAM

Jeremy Irons won the 2007 Golden Globe award for best supporting actor for his role in *Elizabeth I*. In his acceptance speech, he said, "Why is it that the jobs that are the most fun are the ones for which you get the rewards?" His big smile indicated the honesty of this powerful reflection. The three parts of this book, and the explanations, wisdom, and tips packed inside, are designed to help your team gain rewards—both intrinsic and extrinsic—while you have fun with your work and with one another.

Part One explains what constitutes an ESI team, why it is valuable, and how to understand emotional intelligence.

Part Two is the heart of the book. It covers the seven skills that make up ESI. It explores the intricacies of each skill and provides examples of the skill in action and ways to incorporate the skill into your repertoire. It's not rocket science; it's brain chemistry. Much of ESI is rooted in how the brain works and responds to stimuli. Seven skills are essential to an emotionally intelligent team: identity, motivation, emotional awareness, communication, stress tolerance, conflict resolution, and positive mood. These competencies are like the Seven Wonders of the World. They are powerful abilities that can redefine the landscape in which your team operates. Undoubtedly, as you apply them to your team, you'll discover unique ways to incorporate these behaviors to maximize your team's success.

Part Three completes your discovery by identifying what the individual team player needs to bring to the table, what the ESI leader needs to add, and values and ethics central to the integrity required of an ESI team. All of this leads to the extraordinary results you are seeking. Believe it or not, teams seek trust, loyalty, and effectiveness above all, and those drive performance.

What Motivates Behavior?

To be an ESI team, you need to understand what makes teams work together well and how they can become even more productive and rewarding to their members. Building that understanding is a core purpose of this book.

We assert that human behavior is motivated by the desire to improve the quality of life and that teams exist because the tasks that improve the quality of life are often too complex for one individual to accomplish alone. Improving the quality of life means achieving the progressive satisfaction of the needs identified in Abraham Maslow's hierarchy (1943), as depicted in Figure I.1.

Whether you realize it or not, teams strive to satisfy this inherent sequence of needs, just as individuals do. Human beings, and the teams they constitute, naturally move toward satisfying these successive needs and attempt to overcome whatever blocks their satisfaction. So our brief definition of a team is a group of two or more people who interdependently seek to solve problems in order to improve the quality of life. We'll go into much more depth in Chapter One.

FIGURE I.1.   MASLOW'S HIERARCHY OF NEEDS.

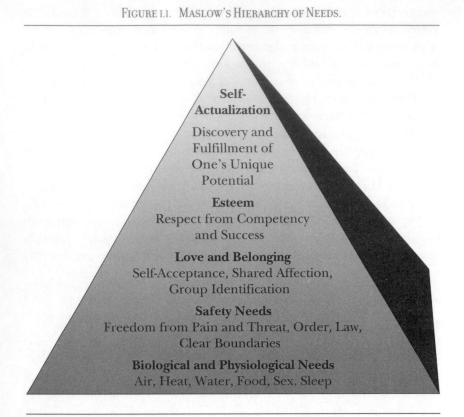

**Self-
Actualization**
Discovery and
Fulfillment of
One's Unique
Potential

Esteem
Respect from Competency
and Success

Love and Belonging
Self-Acceptance, Shared Affection,
Group Identification

Safety Needs
Freedom from Pain and Threat, Order, Law,
Clear Boundaries

Biological and Physiological Needs
Air, Heat, Water, Food, Sex, Sleep

Adapted from Maslow's Hierarchy of Needs.

PERFECTION NOT REQUIRED

These most brisk and giddy-paced times.
WILLIAM SHAKESPEARE

Hanging out on Planet Earth as a human invites the opportunity to learn and grow. every day is chock-full of chances. We invite you to approach each day with the willingness to notice and take advantage of those moments when you can practice the seven ESI skills. practice does make perfect; no individual and no team does it flawlessly the first time or all the time. Practice will create new habits that will gradually begin to change your team's entire experience of itself and the work it performs.

As you continue building your skills, your team will begin to reach a critical mass of competency, at which point there will be a powerful convergence. You will suddenly notice that you move together more gracefully, effortlessly, powerfully.

Along the way, you and your teammates will discover what it takes to be successful at each particular juncture. You may be better at communication than you are at positive mood. Or you may be quite good at aspects of a skill and yet find more room for improvement. Discovery is what it's all about—enjoy the journey.

You and your team have the opportunity to create together a rich and colorful tapestry. This book provides weaving lessons. Get the loom out and get to it!

Note: In order to protect the privacy of the many organizations and individuals we work with, all names are changed in the book.

PART ONE

THE VALUE OF EMOTIONAL AND SOCIAL INTELLIGENCE FOR YOUR TEAM

CHAPTER ONE

WHY EMOTIONAL INTELLIGENCE IS SO VALUABLE FOR TEAMS

All the forces in the world are not as powerful as an idea whose time has come.
VICTOR HUGO

In a compelling *Grey's Anatomy* vignette, Dr. Addison Shepherd, a renowned obstetrician, led multiple teams of doctors as she performed a C-section to deliver premature quintuplets. High-risk pregnancy was putting it mildly, so teams of surgeons were lined up before the births. When it was time, pagers went off all over the hospital, in doctors' homes, on the freeway, wherever the surgical teams were. Many complications were identified before the births. One baby had heart trouble, so Dr. Preston Burke, the heart specialist, was present with his team, whose members were ready to receive the baby immediately and begin what they hoped would be lifesaving work. One had a brain injury, so Dr. Derek Shepherd, the brain surgeon, and his team were ready to roll the minute the tiny infant was handed over. They all worked as a powerfully synchronous team. The whole Surgery Department worked on keeping those babies alive. It looked like most might make it; one didn't.

As intern Meredith Grey was seeking to comfort the new mother, she had a revelation. She hurried to the babies, with the mother trailing her. Meredith picked up an infant who was failing to thrive and put her in the incubator with a sibling, snuggling them right up tight. She told the mother that twins were often put together in an incubator to promote survival: after all, they'd been close together for nine months, and they still needed each other.

Teams abound in this story—the parents, ready to take on and raise these blessed beings, and their siblings ready to welcome them home. The surgery department as a whole was a team at its best, and each specialist team in the Surgery Department was its own impressive team. The most profound team of all was the quintuplets, helping keep one another alive.

When someone you love is having surgery, you want the highest-performing team you can find. Nothing else matters to you but getting the best outcome. Though you may not realize it, you want more than state-of-the-art equipment, evidenced-based best practices, and the most highly trained and clinically competent surgical team you can access. You want a team that hums along like a well-oiled machine. You want a team that can handle pressure. You want a team that can adapt to a rapidly changing environment. You want a team that is abundantly resourceful and resilient. You want a team that is emotionally and socially intelligent.

It's not just surgical teams that need to possess emotional and social intelligence (ESI); all the teams you're on need it if they want to make it anywhere beyond mediocre performance in this global economy, where information travels at the speed of light. In fact, the entire world could use more of it! Almost every part of our daily experience is related to how well teams function. Whether a product is available online or on a shelf is contingent on a host of teams operating well. That backlog in the checkout line at the grocery store is related to team functionality. Getting projects completed on time and on budget, leading innovation in your industry, being perceived as an organizational thought leader, and offering top-notch products and services that meet the demands of your particular marketplace all come down to team functionality.

Fortunately, ESI is based on skills that any team can develop and refine. This creates an enormous opportunity to improve team functioning. No matter how well or poorly your team is operating, there's more potential. There is no glass ceiling on team performance—the sky's the limit!

SIGNIFICANT PERKS FOR TEAMS AND THEIR MEMBERS

A team that functions with healthy emotional and social intelligence experiences a multitude of benefits. Decades of work with organizations and teams repeatedly demonstrate that the relationships between team members affect everyone's productivity and happiness. There's an old saying that you may have heard: "If Mama ain't happy, nobody's happy." Well, the same is true for team members: if one team member isn't happy, everyone is negatively affected. A team with high ESI is happier all around. We make these observations based on our decades of work with teams and the organizational environments they live in. Furthermore, a growing body of research has demonstrated the value of ESI teams. These are some of the benefits:

- Individuals on the team are happier, more satisfied, more creative, and more productive.
- They enjoy working with their team, which reduces defensiveness, opens their thinking capacity, and facilitates creativity. In short, the creative grow even more creative. That's powerful— more solutions drive more innovation!
- They persevere when tackling challenging tasks and complete them when other teams fail. Nothing breeds success like success.
- All of this yields better productivity. That's money in the bank. Return on investment. Bang for the buck.
- For the individuals on such teams, these benefits result in improved emotional well-being and better odds that they'll maintain a good work-life balance.
- The coworkers, friends, and families of people working on ESI teams get an added perk: they have more relaxed, playful, productive, and enjoyable relationships with that team member.
- Organizations also clearly benefit when individuals and teams are happier and more creative. Retention, engagement, and productivity all rise.

- Being happier is related to being healthier, which translates into tangential savings because fewer people call in sick and health insurance costs are mitigated.
- Humanity as a whole benefits when people work well together. Collaborative efforts achieve more efficient resource use and enhance communication, which reduces conflict and supports peace and well-being right here, where you and those you love live.

What Is a Team?

On the news and in conversation, people are always referring to teams: teams of scientists, search and rescue teams, teams of engineers, sports teams, surgical teams, implementation teams, and the ever-popular "teams of experts." Who knows if anyone is really talking about the same thing! The dictionary defines a team as "a number of persons associated together in work or activity," such as a number of persons competing in sports or a group of workers completing a set of operations or "a group of specialists or scientists functioning as a collaborative unit." That broad definition can be better understood when the concept of a team is broken down into key aspects. If your team can clearly define the functions listed here, you have a team. If not, you probably have a group or at best a partly dysfunctional team.

- *Purpose.* A team needs a purpose to exist. It can be stated as the problem to be solved or the result to be achieved. Reportedly, one of the best-selling personal books in recent years is *The Purpose Driven Life* by Rick Warren (2002). People crave purpose, and that's true whether we're looking at our personal or our professional lives. Teams have the same core need; they want to know that they are making a difference, that what they do matters in some way. That's not possible without having a specific mission, a reason to be. The lack of a defined purpose is one of the most likely sources of team dysfunction.
- *Productivity.* A team needs feedback that is clear and useful and needs to know that the work it is doing contributes to the goals of the organization in a meaningful way. Pride comes from a sense of productivity, which is essential fuel for the next

output. A team that feels that it never gets anything done or that the work it does is irrelevant will operate from a discouraged and disempowered space. That's the start of a downward spiral. The discouragement spins the team downward, which eventually leads to poorer results, less creativity, increased disengagement, and higher turnover. There's enough of that already. One of the highest costs organizations pay on health insurance claims is for depression.

- *Numbers.* Two or more people make up a team. Some people argue that a duo is simply a pair and not a team. However, it takes only two to tango, which is a passionate display of teamwork when danced well. In any situation in which individuals are called on to work together and solve problems, the skills and disciplines of collaboration are required, and you have the makings of a team.

- *Longevity.* There is no standard length of time for a team to exist; high-functioning teams last as long as they are needed and not a moment longer. Some teams come together for a very brief moment in time to perform a discrete task that is time-sensitive, and when the task is done, the team is disbanded. Such teams are referred to as just-in-time teams.

One of the ultimate just-in-time teams was born on April 13, 1970, when the number two oxygen tank exploded on Apollo 13, crippling the service module as it lost oxygen and electrical power. Over 200,000 nautical miles from Earth, the crew had to use the lunar module as a lifeboat for most of the flight. It was equipped to sustain two people for two days, yet there were three crew members who faced a four-day trip back to Earth, if they made it all.

The situation was dire. They had only ten hours' worth of power available from the command module. The fuel had to be reserved for the approach and reentry to Earth's atmosphere, and the module had the heat shield essential to keeping the astronauts safe during reentry.

It was an epic fight for survival in an extremely hostile environment. The spacecraft's successful return to Earth was made possible by extraordinary teamwork and ingenuity, led by NASA's chief flight director, Gene Kranz, whose motto was "Failure is not an option." He assembled every available bit of talent he could find. Manufacturers of the main Apollo systems sent their top specialists immediately. Simulators, computer models, and experts were linked into a network and worked furiously to figure out a way to keep the astronauts alive and to get them home. It was an unprecedented display of tenacity, ingenuity, and perseverance, with rigorous attention to every tiny detail, that allowed them to prevail against all odds, just in time. Every single maneuver was tested in the simulators; every calculation was verified with computers.

Ultimately, Apollo 13 had the most accurate landing in the history of manned flight. The mission operations team and the astronauts were awarded the Presidential Medal of Freedom for their heroic actions.

Far less dramatic than the team that came together to prevent the Apollo 13 disaster, yet quite important in an organization's daily life, are the typical senior teams found in most companies. These are composed of the top leaders in the organization and will likely exist as long as the organization exists, although the members of the team will change. As your teams develop more of their ESI skills, they are more likely to function with some of the same focus and commitment to success as the Apollo team or the daily success of an effective executive team.

- *Accountability*. This essential characteristic is closely linked with purpose and productivity. The team must be routinely held accountable. Although accountability is usually managed by a leader on the team or a manager at a higher organizational level, it can be done by the team itself, though that takes considerable commitment to the team's purpose. Accountability functions to keep the team on target, committed to quality, and meeting its objectives. A team with no accountability is an amorphous group, acting more like a bunch of cells swimming around in a petri dish than a single organism. With accountability, you have the opportunity for a high-performing, productive, well-integrated team.
- *Power*. Power in a team is found in two primary forms—authority and influence. Authority is the direct ability to mandate action: it allows the leader to require deadlines, adjust project priorities, and hire and fire employees. Influence is much

more subtle and when used with elegance is almost certain to be more effective. The dictionary defines influence as "producing an effect without apparent exertion of tangible force or direct exercise of command and often without deliberate effort or intent." This is the most potent way to teach, guide, and coach people. It's often the most effective way to move someone from no to yes. Effective use of authority and influence are primary tools in developing the seven skills of emotional and social intelligence in teams.

In assessing your team's power, the questions to ask are who uses authority and influence and how well are those forms of power wielded. Ideally, the leader has direct power and uses it well. However, our experience has shown that there are many situations where an individual is appointed to lead a team but is given no direct power or authority. A team leader who doesn't perform the personnel evaluations for the team members and has no ability to provide meaningful, concrete rewards or consequences for team behavior must be adept at using influence to propel the team to success.

WHAT IS EMOTIONAL AND SOCIAL INTELLIGENCE?

Simply put, emotional and social intelligence reflects the ability to recognize and manage your own emotions and to recognize and respond effectively to the emotions of others. It includes understanding your social community from the "big picture" point of view and the ability to direct change and to adapt to that change.

Emotional intelligence (EI) or *emotional quotient* (EQ) are terms used interchangeably, so you can interpret them as referring to the same concept. ESI adds the vital dimension of *social intelligence,* which the psychologist Edward Thorndike (1920) referred to as the ability to function successfully in interpersonal or social situations. Thorndike's work in the 1920s has been built on by many in the EI world, especially Reuven Bar-On and Daniel Goleman.

Bar-On (2005) outlined the history of the development of ESI and helped define social intelligence when he wrote that "the early definitions of social intelligence influenced the way *emotional intelligence* was later conceptualized. Contemporary theorists like Peter Salovey and John Mayer originally viewed emotional intelligence as part of social intelligence (1990, p. 189), which suggests that both concepts are related and may, in all likelihood, represent interrelated components of the same construct" (p. 1).

While there are many definitions of emotional intelligence in circulation, we have found only one research-based approach that incorporates both emotional and social intelligence in a family of EQ measures. Reuven Bar-On, creator of the Emotional Quotient Inventory® (EQ-i) (1997), emphasizes that one must consider both emotional and social intelligence together. In a 2005 paper describing his model, Bar-On states that "emotional-social intelligence is a cross-section of interrelated emotional and social competencies, skills, and facilitators that determine how effectively we understand and express ourselves, understand others and relate with them, and cope with daily demands" (p. 3).

The fundamental tenets of ESI that influence the efficacy of teams are the following:

1. The ability to understand your own emotions—knowing what you feel and why you feel that way
2. The ability to use your emotions wisely, knowing how to manage and express them intentionally
3. The ability to understand and respect the emotions of others
4. The ability to respond to, influence, and interact with the emotions of others

These four components are always exercised in a social environment, which means that while they have a significant impact on individuals, the impact is even greater for teams. Hence these two additional tenets apply:

5. The ability to recognize that your emotions are applied in a social context, a complex system of relationships that requires sensitivity and tempered responses
6. The awareness that all ESI components come together to influence your ability to respond to and work with change, which is a constant dynamic in the environment

Should We Measure Emotional Intelligence?

One of the first choices when working with EI or ESI and your team is whether to use an assessment to measure emotional intelligence. Of course, teams are made up of individuals. There is value in assessing both individual ESI and team ESI. The three most popular assessments used with individuals are the Bar-On EQ-i®, Daniel Goleman's Emotional Competence Inventory (ECI), and the Mayer-Salovey-Caruso Emotional Intelligence Test (MSCEIT)®. Our own Team Emotional and Social Intelligence Survey (TESI™) works in a complementary manner with each of them.

Whether a team uses a measure or not, the concepts that are central to the most respected instruments are similar and generally accepted in the field. Cherniss (2004) discusses the three most thoroughly researched and popular models and finds many similarities as well as important differences among them. We use primarily the Bar-On EQ-i when working with individuals, although we respect all three. The EQ-i includes five scales and fifteen competencies, and information on these skills can be found in Bar-On's *Technical Manual* (1997). Each of these measures is described in our book *Emotional Intelligence in Action* (Hughes, Patterson, and Terrell, 2005).

The Bar-On EQ-i offers reports to clients that are clear, practical, and excellent as a resource for achieving the sustainable change they are seeking. Also available with the EQ-i is a report that presents a group picture based on a calculation combining the reports of the individual team members. The group report can be combined with our Collaborative Growth Team ESI Survey, which is expressly designed to assess the ESI skills of teams. Based on our decades of research and consulting, we developed this instrument to facilitate team interaction by considering team members' assessments of how the team uses the seven ESI skills. This creates a team 360-degree survey and establishes a well-focused beginning for in-depth team development. We've discovered that when using a combination of instruments, teams tend to generate their own informed and well-targeted strategic discussions. Resistance disappears as team members recognize the validity of each topic and how the skills fit together to affect the experience of being a team.

We find that we can help teams successfully develop their ESI whether we use an assessment or not, although an assessment allows us to more specifically, more quickly, and more thoroughly identify the needs of our clients and choose the focus of team interventions with more precision. For example, we often work with teams in conflict. A typical profile of such a team might show that it is challenged in using communication skills and appropriate conflict resolution tactics on our Team ESI Survey. Although we aren't surprised, this information is often an eye opener for the team. Presenting this feedback, based on the participants' own observations, brings immediate credibility and facilitates commitment, leaving the team more willing to dig in and explore team members' current interactions and skills. This awareness opens possibilities of team improvement, which liberates productivity, inspires team members, and empowers them to become a high-performing, high-flying team that meets its objectives.

WHAT ARE EMOTIONS?

Some managers are uncomfortable with
expressing emotion about their dreams,
but it's the passion and emotion that will attract
and motivate others.
JIM COLLINS AND JERRY PORRAS

Emotion is what guides human choices and inspires behavior, because emotion is the meter that indicates how good you feel about something. It motivates you to act—either so you can stay feeling good or so you can stop feeling bad and start feeling better. It originates from physical sensations that result from the body's innate ability to register and distinguish between pain and pleasure. In this sense, emotion is a direct response that tells you which way to move, and for humans, there are only three or four possibilities. The two fundamental moves are *toward* and *away from*. It's pretty simple: we move toward that which we associate with pleasure, and we move away from that which we associate with pain. This explains why chocolate often prevails over peas! It may also explain why you try to keep your boss happy, why you respond warmly when your life partner brings you flowers or puts the dishes away without being asked, why you use a potholder, why kids disappear when their parents argue, and why you screen your phone calls!

The third move we can make is *against*. When we, as humans, feel that our efforts to move *toward* have been blocked or when we have been threatened (forced to move *away*), we can move *against* the threat or obstacle. This assertion of force is intended to eliminate the obstacle that stops our progress or to eradicate a threat so we can feel safe again.

There is also a fourth option: simply to *stop*, to be still and not move at all. Animals employ this tactic as a survival skill. For example, a rabbit will freeze in its tracks instinctively to avoid being detected by a predator. Humans can learn a thing or two from all creatures, great and small. The option to stop isn't limited to a biological response. It can be used intentionally by individuals who have developed a high degree of emotional intelligence, enabling them to control automatic physiological responses and knee-jerk reactions that come with an emotional experience. One of the best practices to gain competency in this skill has proved to be meditation. Meditation teaches you to direct the focus of your attention away from impulses that are fearful (move away), acquisitive (move toward), or angry (move against) and center it in a neutral, calming rhythm like breathing.

In addition to functioning as directives to act, emotions can function as evaluative responses. Responding requires energy, and while some humans seem to have nearly limitless energy, most of us do not. If we desire something strongly that will not be easy to obtain, it is helpful to experience the emotions of hope, longing, and determination, because those emotions can sustain the efforts necessary to persevere and achieve the desired outcome. However, if we had been hopeful and determined and worked doggedly for a long time without garnering success, those emotions might transform into hopelessness and discouragement. These emotions can be a signal to quit wasting energy on an effort to change something that we simply cannot change.

The truth is that *emotions* are what *motivate* us to action; in fact, both words share the same Latin root, *emovare*, which means "move."

Another term closely associated with the term *emotions* is *affect*. In humans, there is a constant interplay among three inter-related experiences: our basic temperament or disposition, our emotions, and our mood. Reber (1985) presents an interesting picture as he seeks to define emotions in *The Dictionary of Psychology*. Emotions, he says, are "normally acute in that they are relatively short-lived levels of arousal and desires to act," such as fear, joy, and disgust, and they "are regarded as intensely experienced states" (p. 235). It turns out that much of this definition is supported by a consensus understanding based on its use in a particular context. To achieve the full potential of working with a team, it helps to have the members clarify what they mean when they talk about emotions. Moods are somewhat different; they are more persistent emotional states and generally come and go, depending on how an individual has learned to interpret specific circumstances and changes in the environment.

Physiologically, emotions appear to accompany specific chemicals that circulate throughout the body conveying the critical information about which way to move, how hard, and how fast. Did you know that a biochemist's analysis can reveal whether tears were cried out of joy or out of sorrow? It's truly remarkable to think how complex the human heart, mind, and body are; that tears of joy are chemically different from tears of sorrow gives new meaning to the notion that the eyes are the window to the soul.

Candace Pert, an internationally recognized pharmacologist, has made fascinating discoveries and observations about emotions. She was the neuroscientist at the National Institute for Mental Health whose work led to the discovery of the opiate receptor and our understanding of how chemicals enter our body at the cellular level and achieve their effect. Her book *The Molecules of Emotion* (1997) is a delightfully educational story about the discovery and function of neuropeptides. These are the long-chain amino acids that circulate throughout our bodies, serving as "communicator molecules" delivering critical information about how we feel to and from such centers as the heart, brain, and gut. Pert asserts that emotions are the "glue" that holds our cells together and that they are the magical point of interface and transformation where energy becomes information. But our understanding of emotion has not always been so magical and unifying.

The dictionary defines emotion in several ways, including as (1) a physical or social agitation, disturbance, or tumultuous movement and (2) turmoil or agitation in feeling or sensibility. With those kinds of definitions, it is no wonder that organizations used to treat emotions like muddy shoes, expecting employees to "leave them at the door." It's been a slow evolution as organizations have realized that not only is that impossible but it's also detrimental. Dismiss the sorrow and the angst, and out go the joy and passion that play such a critical role in employee engagement and innovation.

Because emotions occur in response to sensations, we like to say that emotions are about what we touch—and not just what we touch with our fingers or our skin but what we touch with our eyes and ears and with our taste buds and with the olfactory nerves in our nose. Emotions are how we feel about what we touch with our imagination, from the dread of a loud, scary noise in the dark to those fifteen minutes of fame when you're at the top of your game and everyone else gets to see.

A highly colorful and interesting presentation of the relationship between emotions is known as the Plutchik model. Robert Plutchik (2001), a psychologist who served at the Albert Einstein College of Medicine and developed a psychoevolutionary theory of emotion, presents a color wheel that demonstrates that emotions flow from a moderate feeling that can progress to extremes—for example, one can move from pensiveness to sadness to grief. On the positive side, the gradation flows from serenity to joy to ecstasy. Science has made tremendous strides in understanding emotions and in expanding the concept of intelligence to include emotional intelligence.

Because the idea of emotional intelligence rose against the backdrop of cognitive intelligence, it's important to clarify some of the distinctions between the two. Cognitive intelligence manages the objective facts of life: who, what, when, and where. In the realm of human behavior, emotional intelligence is concerned with why and in certain cases how. "*Why* did you start diving off the ten-meter platform?" "I wanted to see what it felt like to fly." "*Why* did you come in to work over the weekend?" "I knew how much it would mean to the team if we had an analysis of that data and could get started first thing Monday morning." "*How* do you hold a premature baby that tiny?" "I hold it very gently, but with all of my strength, as if I were caring for the miracle of life itself."

There may never be a final definitive answer to the question "What is emotion?" However, we are certain that it is powerful and personal and present in everything humans cherish and hold most dear.

DEVELOPING YOUR TEAM'S ESI

A desire to develop ESI competencies, such as skills in conflict resolution and motivation, is primarily what motivates team members and practitioners to explore the emerging field of emotional and social intelligence for teams. Our purpose in founding and operating the Collaborative Growth survey is to support teams and individuals in developing sustainable behavior change. For decades now, we've been guiding and observing the development of sustainable change. It's remarkable, powerful, and essential as an investment, but it is seldom easy. This level of change requires strategically focused work, commitment, and sustained effort.

To understand the possibility for your team's improving its skills, we need to distinguish ESI from personality measures and emphasize the benefit of neuroplasticity—the fact that your brain can change. The most widely recognized personality instruments we're aware of that are used with teams are the Myers-Briggs Temperament Inventory®, Emergenetics®, and DISC®. These present a picture of someone's preferences for being extroverted or introverted, preferring social or analytical thinking, and so on, and can be a great help to teams. However, they are focused on presenting a picture of your preferences, and those are not expected to change. They are different from emotional and social intelligence skills.

Both Bar-On's EQ-i and Goleman's ECI measures focus on the expression of abilities, skills, and traits. Traits are individual characteristics that include a genetic component and create some overlap with personality measures. That's the key subtlety— there are overlaps, but these EQ measures are not measuring personality. Emmerling and Goleman (2003) point to some of the scientific work supporting the plausibility that people can improve their ESI skills. They wrote that "findings from affective neuroscience also provide evidence for the potential to develop emotional intelligence competencies. The findings of LeDoux (1996) seem to indicate that although there are stable individual differences in activation patterns in the central circuitry of emotion, there is also pronounced plasticity" (p. 23). The notion of neuroplasticity is exciting, as it indicates that our brain can and does change even after its initial process of growth and development is completed somewhere in our early twenties. The centers of the brain found to have plasticity are the prefrontal cortex, amygdala, and hippocampus, and all these are involved in the perception, use, and management of emotions. Bryan (2006) further referenced LeDoux to demonstrate that this work of behavioral change requires "rewiring" of our brain. Accomplishing that rewiring entails understanding the goal, commitment, and lots of practice! We can change, but we have to really want to if we're going to make it happen.

No doubt, we're at an exciting point in this developing research, but much remains to be learned. It is stimulating to get the proof and technical explanation of what we see regularly— you *can* teach an old dog, er, team new tricks. What's more, there is a tremendous body of research demonstrating that cultivating emotionally and socially intelligent teams makes good business sense.

CHAPTER TWO

THE BUSINESS CASE FOR TEAM EMOTIONAL INTELLIGENCE

Michael, if you can't pass, you can't play.
COACH DEAN SMITH TO MICHAEL JORDAN IN HIS FRESHMAN
YEAR AT THE UNIVERSITY OF NORTH CAROLINA

Individual and team ESI skills have become a mandate for successful organizations. Any business that isn't prioritizing these mission-critical behaviors is at a significant disadvantage, and there aren't many businesses that can afford to give away a competitive edge to a market rival. Although the business case for cultivating these skills is compelling, many organizations are just awakening to this vast potential. Never before have so many pressures been exerted on companies at once, and the solutions for adapting to them all can only be found by evolving an ESI skill set that provides the flexibility necessary to accommodate changing market dynamics. Consider the following points:

- The rapid pace of innovation is demanding a more flexible, more collaborative, more creative workforce.
- The global marketplace and international outsourcing are delivering higher productivity at lower cost.
- A looming talent shortage as baby boomers retire is making companies vulnerable to knowledge gaps and vacant positions.

Technical competencies are no longer the defining attribute of successful organizations. Emotionally and socially intelligent teams are the hallmark of the world's most innovative, most profitable, and most sustainable organizations. Imagine for a moment that an auto manufacturer has given a mandate to two teams to design a car that gets better gas mileage. One team plunges into the challenge, intent on coming up with the most fuel-efficient car ever made. The other team reacts with frustration and anger, feeling, "Been there, done that." These team members are tired of the same old problem. Besides that, sales of gas-guzzling SUVs are exploding.

Which team comes up with the snazziest, most fuel-efficient car? The wild and crazy enthusiastic bunch, of course. No mystery there. The reason it's a no-brainer is that the enthusiastic team has much better ESI skills and behaviors. The difference in outcomes between an optimistic, energetic team and an angry team are as obvious as night and day.

Team interactions are inherently emotional. Professionals working with organizational dynamics and human psychology have been evaluating the effects of emotions on our behavior and performance for a very long time. More recently, that research has been put in the language of emotional and social intelligence. Whether studies have been done explicitly to assess the value of an ESI skill directly or to evaluate behaviors that have long been recognized as critical to team performance, such as constructive conflict resolution or social affiliation, they consistently show the direct impact emotions have on team performance.

Team ESI pays off in measurable return on investment (ROI). The competency approach to ESI has proven to have real economic value for organizations. Lyle Spencer (2001), former president and CEO of the Hay Group subsidiary McBer Company, described in detail the calculations used to determine return on investment from an individual's or team's use of EI skills. For example, he presented data on a self-managing work group team in Hoescht Celanese U.S. plants. He found that superior teams outperformed average teams by 30 percent. As he observed, "Interestingly, the additional 30 percent incremental productivity Hunter et al. (1990) found for individuals in moderately complex jobs appears to hold for teams as well. Teams, however, greatly leverage economic outcomes. The value of team EICs [emotional intelligence competencies]— . . . all of which can be affected by EIC-based selection and team-building training— can be calculated for groups in the same way it is for individuals. Even a 1 percent shift in team performance in this case was worth $98,000—which provides an economic justification for a lot of team building" (2001, pp. 52–53). Don't miss this important point! Focused investment clearly pays off.

The popularity of Patrick Lencioni's book *The Five Dysfunctions of a Team* (2002) is an example of the hunger to expand team performance. The five skills he calls on teams to develop are trust, conflict management, commitment, accountability, and results. Working with the Collaborative Growth model, Lencioni, in Figure 13.1 in Chapter Thirteen, provides a proven path to enhancing these skills so they don't become dysfunctions that derail your team.

ANGER OR POSITIVE ATTITUDE—IT MATTERS

Anger is a powerful emotion that can cause the team members toward whom it is directed to cringe, withdraw, and sometimes shout back. The ESI skills of emotional awareness, communication, and conflict resolution will probably prove most helpful when teams are seeking to deal with anger. When they don't handle it effectively, the consequences can be similar to that reported by Gibson and Tulgan (2002, p. 34), drawing on the research by Pearson, Anderson, and Porath (2000), who studied how employees responded to anger and negativity in the workplace. They found that of the subjects they studied:

- Fifty-three percent lost work time worrying about the incident or future interactions.
- Thirty-seven percent believed that their commitment to the organization declined.
- Twenty-eight percent lost work time avoiding the instigator.
- Twenty-two percent put less effort into work.
- Ten percent spent less time at work.
- Twelve percent changed jobs to avoid the instigator.

These consequences have a harsh impact on the success of business, and their effect is often most pronounced at the team level. Although positive energy can successfully counter anger and negativity at team meetings, all the time spent countering negativity could have been focused on meeting the mandate instead.

Fortunately, the flip side is also true; there are also behaviors that increase positive results. In an article titled "Don't Worry, Be Happy," Kate Sweetman (2001) reports that companies with top teams made up of executives with a positive attitude "had 4 percent to 6 percent higher market-adjusted earning *per share* than companies who did not have these positive teams." Interestingly, it also helps if the team members have similar temperaments. It ups the sense of psychological safety.

FOLLOW THE LEADER

The scope of ESI behaviors exhibited by an organization's leader deeply affects its teams' effectiveness. Researchers at the Center for Creative Leadership (CCL) uncovered telling results (Ruderman, Hannum, Leslie, and Steed, 2001). They compared the relationship between the EQ-i scores and the results from their well-respected 360-degree leadership instrument known as Benchmarks®. The CCL researchers found that out of the sixteen Benchmarks factors, ten were significantly related to the EQ-i subscales. The center also examined why executives' careers derailed. The results showed that a high percentage of careers are derailed for reasons related to emotional competencies, including inability to handle interpersonal relationships, difficulty building and leading a team, and difficulty changing or adapting. Their work, which emphasizes the importance of being able to work with a team, is exactly why you should get busy enhancing your own and your team's ESI skills.

The skills that derail leaders have a harsh impact on team efficacy. Teams in organizations led by leaders or influenced by team members who have low ESI skills are undermined, misdirected, and deprived of the resources and authority needed to do the task at hand. Moreover, leaders who fail to use ESI behaviors often lose their most talented team members.

EI AND TEAM PERFORMANCE

Improving emotional intelligence improves team results. Vanessa Urch Druskat is a leader in developing excellent research to prove it. She and Steven Wolff reported that effective teams need three conditions: trust, group identity, and group efficacy (2001, p. 82). We agree, and our work leads us to amplify these conditions into seven core ESI skills for a team, including identity. Our model, Figure 13.1 in the Results Chapter, demonstrates that the integrated practice of these skills leads to trust as well as other highly desired elements such as loyalty. The integration of these two layers of performance leads to sustainable productivity and emotional and social well-being. Experiencing success at these levels builds an unquestioned sense of group efficacy.

Lynn Offermann, James Bailey, Nicholas Vasilopoulos, Craig Seal, and Mary Sass, all of George Washington University, evaluated the relative contribution of emotional competence and cognitive ability to individual and team performance. They found that emotional competence does have an impact, particularly on team performance, and that impact is greater than cognitive intelligence. They used the ECI-U developed by Boyatzis and Goleman to measure emotional competence (EC). The authors reported that emotional competence "may have greatest relevance to performance in team contexts where the ability to interact effectively with others is a far more critical skill, and . . . this effect is not due merely to the possession of certain major personality traits. . . . There was a significant relationship between total ECI score and performance on the team project, such that teams with higher average EC performed better on the team project" (2004, pp. 235–236). They also found that individual attitudes toward one's team were related to emotional capability. The authors hypothesize that individuals high in emotional competence "are more likely to report greater satisfaction and cohesion in teams because they like teamwork more than those lower" in emotional competence (p. 237). Thus it is important to be aware of the tasks being asked of a team so the right individuals are selected to serve on your teams.

A study by Jordan and Ashkanasy (2006) evaluated the hypothesis that self-awareness, a key aspect of emotional intelligence, affects team effectiveness, "measured in terms of team members' ability to maintain a focus on achieving goals and the effectiveness of the process used to achieve those goals within the team" (p. 150). They focused their study on the EI skill of emotional self-awareness, based on their belief that this is the core EI value for teams. Team members constantly compare themselves with others in their work group, which is one of the reasons that when team members develop emotional awareness, the team performs better. This study did find that self-awareness was strongly related to team effectiveness. Understandably, then, the researchers' advice to managers is "to focus on improving emotional self-awareness as a relatively quicker way to improve team skills" (p. 160).

Hillary Anger Elfenbein, of the University of California–Berkeley's Haas School of Business, evaluated the role of EI on teams by looking at it from two directions: the EI that individuals bring to the table and the group's emotional intelligence as a whole. In addition to reviewing the existing research, she and colleagues considered two groups of teams. One was a group of young people aged seventeen to twenty-three brought together for a year's service with Americorps, the domestic version of the Peace Corps. The other group was composed of teams competing for a prize in Harvard University's M.B.A. program. She found that "groups' emotional intelligence is an important predictor of a range of team-level performance measures, including ratings by senior staff members, retention, and self-reported outcomes such as performance, liking of colleagues, and team learning" (2006, p. 167). Elfenbein's is one of the first works we've seen that does a good job differentiating between the EI skills of the individuals and the EI skills the team develops as a unit.

In working with individual EI, Elfenbein and her colleagues found that teams whose members had higher average EI "reported that they felt greater psychological safety with each other, had lower levels of conflict, made decisions more collaboratively together, and experienced greater team learning over the course of their project" (2006, p. 172). The net result: teams with greater average EI had higher team functioning than groups with lower EI averages.

To evaluate the benefits of the team's EI, Elfenbein interviewed team members, asked questions about successes and failures at work, and prepared a video summary of the interview, which she gave to team members to view and make multiple-choice judgments on the emotion being expressed by their colleagues. A surprising result emerged: the ability to understand other team members' emotional expressions explained 40 percent of the variance in team performance (2006, p. 179). This is a powerful result!

In grappling with the age-old question of what is intelligence, Elfenbein's answer is congruent with ours. She said the "intelligence of a group should be the ability of that group to collaborate and work interdependently" (2006, p. 177). When a team is able to engage emotional and social intelligence to produce its work effectively, it benefits from what we call collaborative intelligence.

Wolff, Druskat, Koman, and Messer (2006) tackled questions on how to build and sustain effective teams. We appreciate their emphasis on building social capital in a team, which they say "represents the value added by the structure and quality of social relationships . . . [and] is jointly held by the parties" (p. 228). They identify group trust and safety, group efficacy, and group networks as the components of social capital.

The authors identify eight norms for a team's emotional competency. What they call norms we call habits, and their norms resonate with the skills described in this book. We agree that groups are social systems and that the interactions between the members of the group create the building blocks of their emotional and social capacities.

FROM RESEARCH TO REALITY

Forget about all that compelling research for a minute and consider "Exhibit G," the government. Yes, even the United States government has seen the light. The U.S. Department of Labor is increasingly listing emotional intelligence behaviors as criteria sought by businesses. As early as the 1980s, a Department of Labor survey showed that for employers hiring teens, IQ wasn't as important as emotional skills. Even fast-food restaurants and retailers are seeking communication ability, self-motivation, teamwork and other ESI skills from their part-time teenage help!

The Secretary of Labor appointed the Secretary's Commission on Achieving Necessary Skills (SCANS, 1991) to figure out what skills young people need to succeed at work. The commission's purpose is "to encourage a high-performance economy characterized by high-skill, high-wage employment." In a report titled *What Work Requires of Schools: A SCANS Report for America 2000,* the commission identified a host of ESI behaviors, including self-management, sociability, self-esteem, responsibility, integrity, problem solving, and creative thinking. These are core skills if these young workers are to develop the habit of effective teamwork.

In summary, substantial research and overwhelming evidence have confirmed that ESI skills are inexorably linked to success. Emotional and social intelligence is vital to a team's success in many ways, ultimately resulting in what we identify as sustainable productivity and emotional and social well-being for teams. It's an exciting time. ESI behaviors are skills. Organizations can control their own destinies by cultivating these skills, by hiring employees who have developed these behaviors, and by making targeted investments in training their teams to excel in the behaviors needed for success.

With 5,633 career assists and over 32,000 points scored, it's clear that not only did Michael Jeffrey Jordan learn to pass, but he and the Chicago Bulls also learned a little about how teamwork yields sustainable performance.

PART TWO

THE SEVEN SKILLS OF A TEAM'S EMOTIONAL AND SOCIAL INTELLIGENCE

CHAPTER THREE

THE FIRST SKILL: TEAM IDENTITY

*I've grown certain that the root of all fear is that
we've been forced to deny who we are.*
FRANCES MOORE LAPPÉ

Our hometown of Denver, Colorado, lost one of its best law firms the day Gorsuch Kirgis folded in 2005 after sixty years of serving the community. Many of our friends worked there—good people. You probably count at least one lawyer among your friends. The lawyers who made Gorsuch Kirgis such a great firm, albeit a difficult name, were folks who left to serve in the governor's office and other key organizations. They were attorneys who helped cities, towns, and districts throughout Colorado grow, treated their constituents well, and were instrumental in facilitating ethical decisions. Gorsuch attorneys cared for one another, took time to have fun, and knew they needed time for their families as well as their legal practice. It was a humane law firm, and that is not an oxymoron.

However, the humanity did not stand up in the face of the bottom-line pressures as big national law firms developed a strong presence; the competition for this midsize firm was just too much. One attorney from Gorsuch, Andrew Cohen, went on to become a legal analyst for CBS News and the *Washington Post*. He wrote an insightful column for the *Denver Post* emphasizing the strong personal ties that originally bound the firm together through economic ups and downs. The team of lawyers developed deep connections with one another. They took time to develop trust and commitment that got them through the challenges that face any business—especially law firms, whose members are helping clients with so many conflicts. Cohen wrote that the "notion of group loyalty withered in the face of the new mantra: the bottom line is the bottom line" (2005, p. 7B). He astutely went on to say that unless "partnerships are based upon more than the pursuit of cash collections, unless the individual partners figure out ways to nurture binding personal and emotional ties, they aren't likely to last nearly as long as Gorsuch Kirgis did" (p. 7B). We second that motion.

WHAT IDENTITY IS FOR TEAMS

Team identity occurs at two levels. First and most important is that the team members identify with the team. They create a personal association and unity with the team. They want to be known as members of the team. You know you've got the first start to team identity when you tell people, "I'm a member of the Marketing Dream Team" or "I'm one of the Sales Superstars."

There also has to be a "critical team mass" so that team members can grab hold and find purchase. No surprises here—this begins with the team name, a team roster, and a defined purpose. So it might be that Sales Superstars has ten members, led by the director of the Sales Department. The team's purpose is to develop a strategic plan and then review compliance, contribute proposed budget numbers for the annual budget, and review monthly how well their sales targets are being hit.

When team members have identified with the team, the team becomes a problem-solving organism that is larger than the sum of its parts. This is the second part of team identity—the team's reputation as a distinct unit with its own personality. When team identity is highly developed, the members will have strong allegiance that is seen in the self-renewing collaborative efforts made by individuals who feel they belong and who feel appreciated for their contributions.

The organization's perspective on the team's personality provides another level of team identity. For instance, Jan, the chief operating officer of a large insurance company, told her tennis partner, Susan, that their Executive Team is well known for being demanding but also for laughing a lot and for having a great sense of humor. They always have some lighthearted moments at their team meetings and at the monthly directors' meeting. Jan is describing part of the personality of the team as it's recognized in her organization. This can be influential to a team's performance and acceptance, so it's worthwhile to understand a team's personality and how it's perceived in an organization. Many teams live up to their reputations, which is deadly for some teams and fabulous for others.

THE SEVEN INGREDIENTS OF TEAM IDENTITY

Lucky number seven. If you're a betting type, put your money on cultivating the seven ingredients that create a vibrant team identity. The team doesn't need to be a perfect blend of these. It's not a soufflé; it's a team. A little more or a little less of the ingredients won't create a flop.

A team integrated into its organization, with defined leadership and these seven qualities, will have all the makings of a strong identity. Here's the list of ingredients:

1. *Sense of purpose.* Teams need to know what they are supposed to do, or they will flounder. They certainly can't feel a sense of accomplishment without an effective ability to measure their success. Although this may seem self-evident, you'd be amazed at how often this is overlooked. This is true for just-in-time teams as well as standing teams. For example, the diversity team could have been formed because someone thought the organization should be paying more attention to diversity. However, the team may be given no specific mandate, no authority, and no budget. People may initially be positive or even thrilled to serve as a member of that team, but their enthusiasm will quickly turn into annoyance without a clarified purpose. Another common example is the all-purpose standing departmental meeting. If your department is meeting regularly because "that's the way it's always been done" and there's no clear agenda or new definitive action

plan, it's in need of an overhaul to regain its perspective and its purpose.

2. *Acceptance of one another.* It's convenient, but not essential, that team members like each other. Every team isn't going to be a lovefest among friends. The nonnegotiable aspect is mutual respect and support among team members. To be effective, they need a positive attitude toward one another as work partners. Besides the fact that disparaging one another is just plain rude, it also causes separations and actively works against the ability to sustain a cohesive effort.

3. *Perception that the team is a distinct entity.* Qualifiers like *sort of, kind of,* and *like* should never apply to teams. A group that is "sort of a team" or "kind of a team" or "like a team" is an imposter team. That type of group cannot gather and sustain the energy it needs to accomplish the task at hand. Achieving team unity requires a clearly defined purpose, since purpose fuels the team. When team members and others discuss an authentic or genuine team, they call it by name and talk about the people on it and what they do.

4. *Commitment.* Whether it's through a secret handshake, a blood oath, or a solemn vow, individuals identify with the team by making a firm commitment. Janice and Jake were both asked to serve on the budget committee for their city. Janice was interested in the opportunity. She knows that the budget is at the foundation of what each part of the city can do to fulfill its function. She was honored to have the opportunity to make a contribution. Janice is identified with the team. She tells people she serves on that team; she might even put it on her résumé. Jake is bored, thinking "Oh, not the budget committee. Everyone just talks about the numbers; only the city council makes the decision. The committee has no power. It will be a waste of my time." Jake did not commit to the team, nor did he add much. Commitment to the team takes the members through the ups and downs, the successes and setbacks.

5. *Pride.* Have you ever seen a pro stadium half-empty as the game gets under way and noticed fans with paper bags over their heads? Those fans are having an identity crisis. They have a lot of ambivalence about whether they want to be

associated with a team that is the laughingstock of the league. There's a serious shortage of pride. It is hard to identify with something if you don't have pride in its existence. If you say you "serve on the policy committee" but that you're "a member of the Purchasing Team," you've said a great deal. Personal association with the team happens when you are proud to be a part of it. Metaphorically, you will wear the team hat.

6. *Clarity about roles and responsibilities.* The team needs agreement on why it exists, which is the sense of purpose already noted. Next, team members need to know their roles or functions and what they are responsible for producing. Without that clarity, they can't get their arms around their relationship to the team sufficiently to create an identity with it. A mature team takes this part of the identity skill further because members are secure enough and flexible enough to be able to shift between leading and following. Marcia was once the attorney for a very large environmental project evaluating building a new dam and reservoir to provide water for metropolitan Denver. She represented more than forty suburban cities and districts who worked with the Denver Water Department in developing the proposal for federal permits and evaluating every little detail. A broad contingent of specialists was involved in the management team, including biologists, hydrologists, geologists, recreation experts, transportation experts, social scientists, and legal advisers. Pete, a Water Department manager, was appointed to chair the committee. Pete was astute enough to realize that when biological questions were raised, such as aquatic or wetland issues, the biologists should lead the discussion. He would defer to them so that the group would gain the benefit of their expertise. Likewise, when her cities' concerns were at the forefront, Marcia led the dialogue. The benefits of Pete's approach were enormous. The meetings ran much more efficiently, the team leveraged expertise, and team members were able to produce sounder decisions because they had better information.

7. *Resilience.* Resilience is a broad and compelling capability. It's the phoenix rising from the ashes or the "Unsinkable" Molly Brown. Individuals and teams that are resilient are profoundly inspiring. Change has become a fundamental part

of doing business in the twenty-first century. It's paramount that teams be able to flex, to bounce and shift as the terrain rumbles under their feet. This includes disbanding the team when it no longer has a specific purpose.

Team members will form their sense of identity using the seven ingredients in a mix that is unique to that team. Since the team is made up of separate human beings, each of those individuals will have a slightly different sense of team identity. Some will lay claim to that identity and never let it go. Others may have a tentative link, particularly if they don't wish to be part of the team or feel uncertain about roles. It's no surprise that the degree to which individuals identify with the team influences its strength and productivity. As the number of people who identify with the team increases, the strength of the team grows.

WHY TEAMS NEED AN IDENTITY

True story: in the sweltering summer of 2003, we attended a learning community gathering in Philadelphia with friends and colleagues from a long-standing leadership development group. This is a community that has been developing over many years as a result of attending a powerful leadership training known as Bringing Spirit to Leadership offered by FGISpirit. Phil, our local host, was the city's chief operating officer (similar to city manager in other cities), and he treated us to an insider's view of the city. We visited halfway houses, a local Chinese restaurant, and the Fourth of July freedom show; most important to us, we were given a day with a little-known wonder woman named Jane Golden.

In 1984, Golden took on a modest six-week youth program for the city. She embraced the herculean challenge of trying to turn a group of "taggers and graffiti artists" into law-abiding citizens. This effort was part of Mayor Goode's Anti-Graffiti Network. The goal was to put a stop to the graffiti that seemed to be exploding everywhere. Jane Golden met with a group of teens who were known graffiti artists and made a pact with them. If they pledged to be an "Anti," (antigraffiti), she would give them structure, training, materials, and city walls to create murals of their own design. They'd also get paid for their work. The only rules were that the new murals had to be positive and free of profanity and all things inflammatory.

Almost overnight, that six-week project transformed into a long-term program that made a transformative difference in the lives of many teens and their communities throughout Philadelphia. Jane's short-term project grew much larger when she was given the gargantuan challenge of painting both sides of the graffiti-covered Spring Garden Street Bridge in just three weeks. The massive job involved over one hundred teens. Golden described how the people loved the project, "The kids were seen as heroes. I remember people pulling over and stopping traffic on the bridge, beeping and waving, and the kids taking bows. Really, it wasn't about art, it was about the fact that kids were doing something productive for their community" (Golden, Rice, and Yant Kinney, 2002, p. 34). More than two thousand murals were painted under her program's direction.

The story of team identity with these murals is multifold—it's about identity for those young people. It's also about expanding the identity for the neighborhoods that received a beautiful wall that told some of their story and created so much neighborhood pride. It's about identity for Jane Golden, the people in the program, and the city administration as the program survived decades of ups and downs.

Many of those kids faced extremely limited futures; it was all too likely they'd die young and in jail. Being a part of the program meant they had to make a commitment, beginning with signing the antigraffiti pledge. They learned about discipline and responsibility, and they began forming a deeper sense of their own identities and values. Instead of being renegade taggers, they were paid city workers, and their work was valued. They were part of a team they loved. They made a commitment to the team, they had defined responsibilities within the mural project, and in exchange, many were provided with formal art training, assigned to projects that contributed to the community, and earned money. It wasn't easy. Rocco Albano, a writer known as PEZ and NOT (for Number One Terrorist), reported that "graffiti was inextricably intertwined with drugs and alcohol." He said his "addiction to graffiti" was harder to kick than his addiction to drugs and alcohol (Golden, Rice, and Yant Kinney, 2002, p. 35).

These mural teams probably seem a lot different from most of the teams you're a part of now, but they had strong components of the seven ingredients it takes to forge a team identity. We suspect that anyone who was on one of those mural teams looks back at that experience with pride. It was a once-in-a-lifetime opportunity.

You may be able to recall a team that was important to you when you were young. For James, it was his Scout troop, where he worked his way through the ranks from Wolf to Eagle Scout over the course of time from third grade through high school graduation. For Marcia, it was ten years in 4-H and many high school clubs including the local chapter of the National Honor Society. The training you received when you were young laid the foundation for your contributions to teams in your adult life. If you were fortunate enough to have had the opportunity to be mentored by a role model you respected and participate in a program, sport, hobby, or extracurricular activity, you got a good foundation that is almost certainly stronger than the foundations of young people who didn't have such opportunities. It helped form your personal identity, which is part of what it took to get you where you are today. Draw on this background to support your team.

HOW THE TEAM APPLIED THE SEVEN INGREDIENTS

No team is perfect, and that included the mural team. Yet the team has an incredibly impressive performance record. It created *thousands* of murals, each one a project in itself. The work transformed the lives of many of the team members. Think about it: Jane Golden took a bunch of angry teens, trapped in dire circumstances with bleak futures, and created an extraordinarily successful team. How did she do it?

It's all in those seven ingredients of identity; many of them were a part of the team members' experience. Some felt all seven strongly and had a very strong identity with the team; others held back. They did some work with the team but weren't willing to identify strongly with the team. Jane Golden, the manager, certainly described every ingredient being present as a large force in her life.

Team members had a sense of purpose. The team was instantly able to understand the mission. Take a space, create powerful art relevant to the neighborhood while receiving additional art training, and get paid for their efforts. It was very clear when they'd accomplished the goal—there was a spectacular work of art where none existed before.

We can't say with certainty how many members of the mural team accepted one another. Certainly, Golden was well accepted, and she reciprocated that respect. It was an unusual team, and some city officials were conflicted regarding their involvement. Given the youthfulness of the team members and their circumstances and struggles, we suspect that the degree of acceptance among team members varied. But it's clear that they accepted each other to a significant degree, or they would not have been able to complete so many assignments.

The project had an official title, budget, and purpose. It was perceived as a distinct entity.

The commitment of Golden and her staff was strong. Many of the artists shared that commitment, some with zeal. Others hung back. The team members had various levels of commitment.

Pride for the team's work and for being on the team is one of the central reasons it was so successful. The art itself is stunning, and team membership was a core part of changing some young people's life track from jail to meaningful employment.

Creating defined roles and responsibilities, Golden reported, was one of the important lessons the team learned.

BENEFITS AND DOWNSIDES TO CREATING TEAM IDENTITY

These skills are crucial to developing a high-performance team, yet any good thing can be taken to an extreme, thereby creating liabilities as well as benefits. Several benefits of this ESI skill are discussed here, and the risks of taking this skill too far are noted.

- *Team identification creates energy.* Do you identify with your team or teams? How do you know? Do you tell people about your team and your role on the team? This identification creates the connection that gives you the energy it takes to show up with a good attitude, participate, and be willing to confront decisions or attitudes when necessary for the good of the team or its purpose. Identification is an energy creator. Without it, you're likely to participate only because you should. You'll be filling your time without creating value for yourself or the team, and you'll almost certainly be cynical.

- *Team identification helps you focus your capacity for action.* It's likely that you are a part of more than one team. If so, do you identify with each team? Of course, some will have more importance to you or your employer than other teams, but if you're on a team with which you don't identify, you are incapable of taking powerful action. You're likely wasting your time and your organization's time.

We work with many senior teams and executive committees. Most people on those teams head a department and serve on many project teams or committees. If this describes you, it is important that you claim or acknowledge a specific identity with the senior team. Think of your teams as each giving you a different-colored hat—red from your department, blue from the interdepartmental strategic plan committee, green from the budget committee, and turquoise from the senior team. (We've proposed this idea for years but haven't had an organization take us up on it yet.) If you put your turquoise hat on when you attend the senior team meetings, it will help you be clearer about your loyalty to that team. It will help you focus on asking critical, clarifying questions about how much certain issues should be discussed with the staff, and it will help you catch yourself when you're about to reveal to your assistant director information that you had committed to confidentiality within the senior team.

We work with the executive team of an organization of about two thousand people. Every year, this team agrees to foster loyalty and openness with one another by keeping sensitive discussions within the team. No matter how earnest they are in the discussions, one person inevitably breaks that promise and talks to someone outside the group, thinking that this person will keep it private. That doesn't happen. It never does. What does happen is something like this.

The Head Wizard of Department D, an executive team member, tells his Number Two Guy some info because they've always been buddies. However, the Number Two guy works out with another senior team member, the Chief Genius, and regularly shares with the Chief what he's heard about the discussion. The Chief happens to be second in command, so she has organizationwide responsibilities rather than one department to run. The Chief's primary loyalty is to the executive team. She believes the ability to have frank and in-depth discussions is critical for the organization's success, and this doesn't happen unless the members trust that what is said there stays there. The Chief feels betrayed when she hears Department D's Number Two Guy chatting about matters she considers highly confidential. The Head Wiz doesn't know about the Number Two Guy's chatting, but even if he did, he may not think anything of it. His primary loyalty is to running his six-hundred-person department. He believes that it's nice to participate in the executive team, but not much really gets done there. His real job is running his department. On a scale of 1 to 10, low to high, the Head Wizard's identification with the Executive Team is about 3. The Chief's is 10. Their perceptions about what constitutes loyalty are different. And that leads to clashes and can diminish trust.

An executive team almost always needs high-level trust and professionalism. That means that every team member must have an explicit identity with and loyalty to the team, even if he or she has a closetful of team hats. However, the Chief also needs to understand the reality of divided attention and multiple loyalties. If the Head Wiz doesn't run his department well, he'll lose his job and not be on the executive team.

It takes sophisticated communication and awareness to manage the realities of divided loyalties when you have different key positions within one organization. These are an important part of your ESI skill base. How authentically and easily you apply those competencies on your team depends on the degree of identity you deliberately develop with your team.

- *Team identity facilitates meaning.* Finding meaning in your contributions, be it a team at work or at church or in the summer sports league, is a core human need. The human species is universally wired to value using its gifts and talents in a way that is purposeful. It's important to know why your team exists and that it matters in some way. It could well be impossible to feel that your contributions are meaningful if you don't feel connected. You must have a sense that you're a part of the team before you can own the results from your contributions and those of your team as a whole.

- *Team identity contributes to loyalty, trust, fun, and cohesiveness.* Your sense of identity with the team enables you to feel ownership in the work the team does and the results the team achieves. This fuels a cycle that increases your loyalty to the team, and that in turn provides motivation to put forth your best efforts, which helps create results, and the cycle continues. Trust starts building, and the team begins to have more fun. Healthy teasing can't happen unless there's an underpinning of trust and affinity for one another. It also creates a cohesiveness that makes it all come together.

- *But don't get carried away!* Some people can get so involved in the team that they forget themselves. This can lead to blind loyalty, with several adverse consequences. You may find that your ability to make good choices or to balance your personal and professional lives is challenged. You may find yourself working at 10:00 PM. You also might like the team so much the way it is that you resist change, or you may become jealous of or resistant to others who want time from the team.

IDENTITY AND UNDERSTANDING

> *I not only use all the brains that I have, but all that I can borrow.*
> WOODROW WILSON

Positive identity with your team can happen only when you have at least moderate pride in being associated with the team. Positive feelings about your team require understanding and acceptance of your teammates. Recognition of the tremendous value experienced when teams grow in understanding, appreciation, and acceptance of one another is the impetus behind the growing interest in team-building workshops and exercises.

If attending team gatherings seems less preferable than going to the dentist, do whatever you can to figure out what makes those unusual beings on your team tick. One of the best ways we've found to gain that kind of insight is to use a personality measure with a team. This provides a nonthreatening way to expand everyone's awareness. Commonly used personality measures are the Myers-Briggs Type Indicator®(MBTI), Emergenetics,® and DISC®. All are self-report measures intended to help people understand themselves and others on their team. The information helps people understand their preferences and those of their teammates and should be presented in a manner such that people recognize there are no right or wrong answers, just different normal human preferences. For example, the MBTI addresses the tendency to be extroverted or introverted. Some people prefer to speak immediately (extroverts); others need time to think things over before they can comfortably discuss matters of importance (introverts).

A strong team is composed of people with differences who understand how to maximize the benefits of holding different perspectives. It takes work to become a strong team. Imagine a team composed of only extroverts—they'd all be talking at once! Who will do the listening? A team built exclusively of introverts will have quiet, short meetings and possibly leave key items unexplored. When team members understand the value of their differences, they can exploit the opportunities of asking the extroverts to get them going and to initiate thinking of alternatives to the issue being discussed. The team can then turn to the more reflective members for observations such as "What's missing?" and "Are we trying to deal with too much at once?" The MBTI presents information to individuals based on their preferences in four sets of opposite pairs, including the extrovert–introvert pair.

Emergenetics is a brain dominance profile that we find particularly effective as a team-building tool. It helps the team understand why Justin just can't stop thinking of new ideas because of his conceptual brain and why Lana is impatient with these distractions. Her structural brain wants to get the first job done well before she takes on something else. Teams benefit when we combine this Emergenetics information with ESI data because they provide different and complementary information. Personality measures primarily reflect attributes of ourselves that are likely to be permanent; ESI focuses more on skills or competencies that can be developed and modified. Using a personality measure and the Team ESI Survey together creates a great one-two approach with a team. With that information in place, team members are ready to increase their skills in targeted areas and build their appreciation of one another.

One of the most important parts of social intelligence is embracing diversity. And that is a big topic! Diversity includes the obvious big three—racial, ethnic, and gender differences—but it also includes differences in thinking preferences, skills, values, and other matters. Combining personality and ESI information is a great way to give teams concrete information on how to expand their capability to work dynamically with diversity. Diversity is a crucial aspect for teams. We'll just emphasize the importance of incorporating your ESI with all the other ways you have of understanding your teammates.

TEAM STAGES AND ESI

Teams function in stages. They come together, figure out ways to be effective, have conflicts, and, if they are functioning well, address and grow from those conflicts and move to a more mature stage of accomplishing their objectives. In 1965, Bruce Tuckman published an article identifying four stages of group development—forming, storming, norming, and performing. These four became the popular way we discuss a team's development. In 1977, he and coauthor Mary Ann Jensen added a fifth stage, adjourning.

The manner in which a team applies its ESI is heavily influenced by its developmental stage. Tuckman's respected work provides a quick sense of how groups develop that is useful to consider in the context of evolving a team's ESI. However, there are differences as well. His research was based on *groups,* many of which were not teams. It included therapy groups and laboratory groups, as well as what might be teams as we have defined them in Chapter One. No doubt teams that have a specific function, such as to provide strategic direction for their organization, are considerably different from therapy groups. Nevertheless, there are similarities. So let's consider the stages and how they relate to forming the ESI skill of identity.

Many teams go back and forth among the stages of storming, norming, and performing. The beginning of a team is a formative stage that is relatively stable in its timing, as is the final adjourning stage. Once a group gets through the formative stage, it is not unusual to find it in a storming mode as various members test the boundaries to learn how much they actually need to comply with the restrictions on their creative freedom. They could also first go into the normative stage, particularly if they're on a just-in-time team that already knows how to work together from prior experience or, like the Apollo 13 team, one that is so committed to the task that storming isn't necessary. In such cases, the normative stage could be quite short as the team jumps right into the performing stage. Although the adjourning stage is usually straightforward, complications can arise if someone is overidentified with the team and just doesn't know how to let go.

Table 3.1 presents some of the emotions and actions that might surface when a team progresses through the various stages.

TIPS FOR GROWING YOUR TEAM'S IDENTITY

- Develop vision and mission statements at a team-building retreat, and hold regular ceremonies to reinvigorate them. Don't treat your vision and mission as things to check off your list and forget. Use this as the way to anchor your team identity. The vision is your lofty statement. In the big picture, why do you do what you do? How will the team make a difference? The mission statement should describe behaviors you commit to in order to accomplish that vision.
- Use a team or organizationwide survey to ask every member of your team or organization about issues relevant to effective operations and well-being. Normally, these surveys ask about satisfaction with pay and benefits. While those factors are important, we recommend that you go deeper. Find each individual's perspective on how well the manager supervises, how well conflict is handled, and if each person's work-life balance

TABLE 3.1. POSSIBLE EMOTIONS AND ACTIONS AT EACH STAGE OF TEAM DEVELOPMENT.

Stage of Development	Possible Emotions	Implications for Creating Identity with the Team
Forming	Hope, excitement, anticipation, anxiety, caution	There may be an eagerness to be a part of the team such that identity is formed rapidly, even prematurely, as depth of understanding and relationships are not yet fully formed. Or there could be considerable caution and holding back, withholding commitment "until I understand how this works."
Storming	Resistance, hostility, silence, passive-aggressive behavior, overcompensating, collaborative or cooperative spirit	This is the conflict stage. Team members willing to work on the conflict with a cooperative or even collaborative attitude will engage their capabilities to resolve the concerns. Those whose attitudes are polarized at one end of the spectrum or the other—silence or aggressiveness—will take the team toward that extreme to the extent they are able. The behaviors of this stage will show up periodically during the life of the team, sometimes in an obvious way, sometimes more subtly.

Norming	Calmness, desire for commonality, satisfaction, curiosity, intrigue	This is the most likely stage in which an honest sense of identity with the team can develop based on a depth of knowledge. Some members will hold back, doing their job but never aligning with the team, so they'll never develop an identity with the team. That doesn't mean the team will be second-rate; as long as there are enough team members who demonstrate enthusiasm and energy, the team can work well. But without the full engagement of a majority of the group, influence and productivity will be compromised.
Performing	Happiness, well-being, boredom, engagement	Most members of a high-performing team will develop a significant identity with the team, to varying degrees. The person who lives for his or her work could become overidentified. The person who likes work but saves a lot of energy for family, community, or projects will identify at a more moderate level.
Adjourning	Nostalgia, depression, relief, satisfaction, pride	Team identity should end at this stage, though memories of the group could remain strong. Team members who resist the adjournment could experience anger and depression.

is respected. The measure we use is the Benchmark of Organizational Emotional Intelligence (BOEI) created by Steven Stein and others at Multi-Health Systems (see Stein, 2007). Be sure to follow up once your team takes the survey. Examine the results, decide on a strategic response, and then follow through. Teams become dispirited more by lack of feedback and follow-through than just about anything else.

- Have each team member around the table tell what the team means to him or her and what he or she wishes it would become. Listen with curiosity and interest, seeking to learn and understand. Take your time; don't rush. Serve refreshments, create a casual atmosphere, and—make it fun!

CHAPTER FOUR

THE SECOND SKILL: MOTIVATION

Even if I knew that tomorrow the world would go to pieces, I would still plant my apple tree.
MARTIN LUTHER

Lupe, now in her late fifties, had sampled a real taste of satisfaction when she created a company that used her strong analytical and marketing skills to help automobile parts companies sell aftermarket accessories. Along the way, Luisa and Jonathon had joined her, and they operated smoothly together as the company's leadership team. Over time, they built a moderately successful company employing twenty people. Then Lupe's analytical skills started waking her up at night. She knew that the company could grow considerably but that they would need to recruit a new and very different type of leader. She brought the question to the leadership team, and the three spent hours wrestling with it. If they brought in a high-profile leader to grow the company, they would have to offer that person a financial interest in the company, and their own roles as leaders and their small collegial environment would change—radically. Is that something they really wanted?

Lupe, Luisa, and Jonathon decided to rent a conference room at a quiet resort a hundred miles from home where they would have two days to explore the possibilities. They questioned their motivation to expand and examined how they would make ends meet if they did not. Could they all embrace the same decision? As co-owners, their corporate bylaws required that any decision to change the structure of the company be unanimous. Luisa was eager to bring in new blood and grow. She was in her sixties, was thinking of retiring in a few years, and wanted to make more money. She also knew she thrived on change and, frankly, was feeling a little bored. Jonathon took the opposite view at the beginning. He liked to play things safe and had always felt unsettled by Luisa's penchant for change. Things were working fine; why take the big risk of bringing a stranger in? He was single and lived simply, so he didn't need more money. Besides, he was in his early forties and envisioned working for another twenty years or more. He sought to keep things as they were because it supported his sense of safety. It seemed to him too big a risk to bring in an unknown and change the whole company.

Lupe was in the middle. She was proud of creating the company and of its success. She remembered the thrill of starting it up and of growing the business; she'd worked very hard to get to this point. However, she was still working hard, and retirement was sounding better and better. And she was excited at the prospect of bringing the company to a whole new level. During their team discussions, Lupe realized that securing her legacy, gaining increased financial stability so that she didn't have to work so hard, and the challenge of growth were most important to her.

The team challenge was to embrace one decision. The three partners explored various possibilities and eventually came to realize that many of their motivations coincided, even though they seemed different initially. No one wanted to sell a part of the company to a person they didn't trust, so Lupe and Luisa commended Jonathon for his concern and asked him to lead the evaluation of the candidates they might consider. As Jonathon began to feel more comfortable, he realized he held a deep regard for his teammates. He knew they had different financial concerns than he did, and he wanted to support them. And when he took an honest look at the situation, he recognized that a company of their small size might not survive in what was becoming a highly competitive market. Jonathon decided that increasing the financial possibilities would be a good thing.

Gradually, a collective vision emerged, and the team decided to seek a new partner who had the skills and passion necessary to take the company to a new level. However, no final decision would be made unless all three agreed on the candidate's qualifications and emotional fit. They unanimously committed to preserve their strength as a team and to embrace the change and vibrancy a new partner would bring. And no one balked for an instant at the potential for significantly increased revenue.

WHAT MOTIVATION IS FOR TEAMS

Motivation is your team's commitment to mobilize its three basic resources: time, energy, and intelligence. That's really all you've got. And none of these has any value without motivation. It is the internal state of each team member that drives your team to execute its plan of action. *Motivation* shares the Latin root *emovare* with *emotion*. It means "*move!*" Getting a team to move is obviously essential, and it's actually easier than you think. But getting each person to work in concert with the rest of the team so that the team can move forward together at the right pace in the right direction at the right time—that requires some real determination and skill. It's not all that uncommon for one team member to be in motion toward the goal while another is moving away from it and a third member of the team is actually moving against it. Agreeing on one goal is critical, and it requires clarity about why your team needs to be motivated.

Many goals require your team to get on the same page and to act in concert. How much commitment each team member feels for each goal needs to be expressed if you want to get results. There's no cookie-cutter approach for creating motivation. So you ask must yourself some serious questions:

- Do you want to be a better team overall?
- Do you want to accomplish a challenging assignment?
- Do you want to breathe new life and energy into a stale team?
- How well do you respond to change? Could you do better?
- How well do you deal with conflict? Could you do better?
- Do you want to create something new?
- What else do you want your team to do?

Knowing what you are seeking is a mandatory first step toward success. "What's in it for me?" (WIIFM) and "What's in it for my team?" (WIIFMT) are mandatory questions you must answer before you'll ignite sustainable motivation. Effective motivation will only arise out of a combination of individual and collective team commitment. People can fake interest; it happens every day. However, true interest is a result of individuals and their team having a concrete sense of why they are doing what they are doing. WIIFMT can include individual rewards, such as recognition or financial benefits, or the reward might be extrinsic, such as feeding hungry children around the world. Whether it's an extrinsic (objective) reward or an intrinsic one (such as internal gratification or well-being), the members of your team will be motivated if they can feel and see and hear the value of the new vision pulling them forward out of their current less-than-optimal situation.

Curiosity and excitement about new possibilities are certain to move a team forward if it is seeking to take the next step up in performance. Members of this team might start to catch fire when they remember how good it felt to master their current level of skills for the first time—the recognition, the accolades, the success! Helping them recapture that feeling can spark the imagination, creating a plausible way to achieve it again. This team needed to reaccess the physical and mental memories of how good it feels to achieve something new and innovative—but it requires a strategic plan to guide and support the forward motion.

If you want a team to take on change that might be threatening or to deal with painful conflict, you may well have to prove why it's worth going through the difficult times that will follow. We worked with a design company whose owner was considering opening a new store in a different state. The staff already had trouble acting like one team; how could the owner motivate them to get along and to step up to the challenge of growth? Leading the staff through specific exercises and assessments gave them a better understanding of themselves and one another. They realized why they were choosing to behave as they did and became more willing to honestly evaluate the ways in which they might be willing to change. But that required the next step: the desire to change. This happened when the owner, Natasha, dramatically and passionately painted her vision and demonstrated concretely how each member of the staff would benefit. There would be new creative challenges requiring technological innovations for operating the stores through a linked Web site. They would also have to develop novel strategies to get current customers to make recommendations in another city. These folks love to be creative! That was the hook to get them more involved. The change process motivated one person to recognize and admit she wasn't a good fit for that organization. Her leaving helped the team become much more cohesive.

THE SEVEN INGREDIENTS OF TEAM MOTIVATION

People do what they do for many reasons: because they seek the rewards of bringing their passion to life, having power and influence, or creating an inspiring legacy. Finding the motivation to go after these goals involves a combination of the following seven ingredients.

1. *People.* Since motivation is an internal state that drives people to action, motivated individuals provide the energy that gets harnessed for the team's success. The ideal is for an entire team to feel highly motivated in a way that can amplify each individual's motivation. Because motivation is derived from individual motivation, it can build and integrate into the dynamic synergy that results in a unique and even more powerful team.

2. *Needs.* At the most basic level, all team behavior is directed toward satisfying a specific hierarchy of needs, which is common in all human beings. Abraham Maslow's research established the five-stage sequence of needs (depicted in Figure I.1 in the Introduction) that humans are driven to satisfy in ascending order: biological and physiological needs, safety needs, love and belonging, esteem needs, and finally, self-actualization. Each member of your team is always functioning to satisfy a need somewhere on that continuum.

3. *Desires.* In addition to specific needs, you and your teammates are also motivated by desires—ideas and experiences that

you want and seek to acquire or develop but are not actually needed for survival. The key unifying motivator for a team is to add value. If your team is down in the dumps, lacking motivation, team members have to gain a sense that their work is meaningful to become motivated.

4. *Goals.* Team behavior is motivated by the goals that individual members intend to achieve and the problems they set out to resolve. These are similar to the big-picture targets that organizations set forth in their vision statements in order to direct everyone's attention toward achieving the same goal. People are motivated by an endless variety of goals, but some that figure most significantly in team motivation in the workplace include respect, recognition, independence, influence, responsibility, advancement, and, perhaps most important, adding value.

5. *Accountability.* Knowing the goal, marking progress, and understanding how the goal will be measured create the possibility for meaningful accountability, and it's a critical aspect of motivation. When accountability works, it's a matched set: the individuals on the team assume responsibility for defining performance and behavioral standards and are held responsible for accomplishing them. The same discipline is required at the team level. Performance and behavior standards are established for the team, possibly by the organization and the team itself. The team then holds itself accountable, just as officials in the organization do. If no one is tracking progress, benchmarking the efforts, and counting on the results, there is much less incentive to perform.

6. *Reinforcement and Rewards.* The enjoyment you feel when you satisfy a need and the disappointment you experience when your actions are unsuccessful both serve to encode your memories with pleasure or pain. This includes team memory, which has a life of its own, just as much as individual memory. That pain or pleasure realistically grounds your expectations of future consequences. Sometimes you or your team are motivated to pursue the intrinsic kind of rewards where the value received comes simply from completing the work itself. At other times, external acknowledgment is essential to reinforce a behavior.

In the workplace, strategies like bonuses, gift cards, paid time off, promotions, public praise, and other external rewards are great assets for motivating employees and teams. A team told it can take next Friday off, with pay, if the project comes in ahead of schedule is given enhanced motivation for teammates to support one another.

7. *Persistence.* To be successful, you and your team must be inspired, coaxed, or cajoled into persevering, no matter how boring or difficult or exhausting the task may be. Teams that work together have a huge advantage over individuals in this category. When one person's energy is flagging, the others can jump in with the inspiration needed to get the juices flowing again.

WHY TEAMS NEED MOTIVATION

Without a real motivation to engage the problems that make up the work we do and exert the full effort necessary to resolve them, nothing gets done well! But the process of solving those problems can be long and boring and just plain hard work—why would anyone want to make the effort? Our species tends to be lazy and clever—and deceptive when someone else wants us to do something we have no personal incentive to complete. Part of the challenge in working with teams is learning how to discover what gives teams and their members a feeling of incentive and ownership so they want to spend the time and make the effort that it takes to succeed.

One of the most effective ways to motivate your team is to *show* team members what it looks like to feel motivated—show them what you want *their* behavior to look like. Model the enthusiasm and determination that you want them to express. To a large extent, motivation is an emotional experience, transmitted through resonance, not instruction. If you are not motivated yourself and cannot supercharge the emotional field in your workplace with that quality of presence, it's going to be tougher to inspire the people who work with you.

Your choice of language will also be a large factor in your effectiveness as a team motivator. Use language that is optimistic, colorful, and punchy. Use fresh descriptions; have a brainstorming session in which you translate the goals of your current project into completely different words. The goals of your current project should be written down. It's hard to hit the target if you can't see what you're shooting for, so write out the goals that have to be accomplished in order for you to be successful—and do this in several different ways. Write them in terms of the most accurate and concise description you can come up with. Then write them with specific attention to the sensory components—what you will see, what you will feel, what you will hear that will be different when the project is successfully completed.

Help all team members get the sounds of their voices active in the room. Craft an agreement together that everyone can support and then have each person individually read it aloud with as much enthusiasm as he or she can muster. This will accomplish at least two things: first, everyone will be on the same page about what the target is and how to hit it, and second, you'll discover right away whose commitment is shiny and polished and dauntless and whose is dragging and lackluster.

Motivation is an emotional activity, and emotions and emotional energy have been misunderstood and demonized since rational science was "liberated" from the superstitions of the Dark Ages and the purview of the medieval Catholic church. It was a dark day for emotional intelligence when the cortex of René Descartes uttered, "*Cogito ergo sum*" (I think, therefore I am).

At first, his limbic brain thought he was kidding and just putting on airs to be funny, and it laughed out loud. But as this pretension continued, it objected vigorously. "Wait a minute, Mr. Cortex; I'm the one who allocates all the energy you get to think with. Are you sure you really want to make such an extravagant claim?"

But his cortex was rapidly becoming so enamored with itself that it really had little to say to the likes of the limbic structure, and from there on it would speak only to other cortexes—preferably the left hemisphere at that!

As the home of the rational mind, the neocortex is the source and repository of our symbolic representations of our sensory world. This is the brain system that acts like a lens to objectify our concrete experience, gives us distance from it, and allows us to reflect on it. But our thoughts "about" the world are by nature fundamentally different and in fact divorced from the sights, sounds, tastes, smells, and feelings that actually motivate us. These are what we experience as the world that we continuously manipulate and grapple with in order to give it the shape and features we have concluded will best satisfy our needs and our desires. (Success in this is the EQ competency called problem solving.)

The neocortex and rational mind are what we use to innovate and to imagine new solutions to the problems in our life. We might not like the way the color of the room "looks" or the way our team meetings "work" or the amount of compensation we received for our efforts, so we imagine and figure out a solution to the problem. But how do we recognize that these are problems in the first place? That is not a rhetorical question! We have to consciously articulate the subtle nuances of our sensory and emotional awareness in order to label any experience with the "move toward" or "move away from" feeling it takes to recognize the situation as a problem *or an opportunity*. Thus the more sensitively we engage both our internal and external states, the more accurately we can discern what it is we are actually being motivated to address.

Thus when we receive messages like "the walls *look* drab," "our team meetings *seem* slow and disorganized," or "our paycheck *feels* inadequate," these are actually alerts that are engaging us emotionally at some level. If we fail to recognize them as such and try to process them as exclusively rational decisions, we will act without the full complement of information that is available to us!

BENEFITS AND DOWNSIDES OF MOTIVATION

The benefits of motivation are innumerable. In one sense, life as we know it is the direct result of motivation in action. This is true for all creatures but particularly for human beings. Elephants will wait for the slowest member of the group. They choose to stay together, motivated to protect the weakest among them. The ability that every biological organism has to register signals from within itself or the environment and be aroused to respond to them in a way that increases the likelihood of its survival is nothing short of a miracle.

We human beings take this a step further in that we are born with the answers to millions of generations of our ancestors' questions encoded in our genes. These answers surface as instincts or preprogrammed behavior patterns, which have proved highly successful in furthering the survival of the species. In humans, these are more like behavioral boundaries rather than discrete responses, and within those boundaries, a great deal of individuality can be expressed due to the differences in our environment and learning. When you combine individuality with the ability to read the environment, your teammates can register signals from one another and their complex physical and financial environment to mesh the excitement of possibility with the practical steps that accomplish team goals.

The downside of motivation is that too much of it can narrow your focus to a single goal so much that tunnel vision on that single outcome blocks the ability to process other important information. Too much motivation can actually become a stressor and lead to burnout. In addition to learning how to keep your team's eyes on the prize, it is essential to learn how to let go, kick back, and coast so that you can recharge your batteries and get motivated again.

THE MOTIVATION OF SOCIAL PAIN

As children growing up, you learned to navigate toward safe and satisfying experiences and away from what was painful by the emotional "highlight reel" contained in your memories. Sometimes it takes multiple unpleasant experiences to trigger a cautionary warning, and sometimes just a single encounter is so impactful that warning sirens are triggered when the slightest sensation calls up that memory. This is how you learn that fire can burn, that late projects have consequences, that new sales have rewards, and that requests from spouses to pick up after ourselves should be heeded. You use these triggers to generate behavior that is unconsciously designed to minimize the risks associated with unpleasant emotions.

As you grew older, you got pretty good at avoiding burns and shocks and falls, but another kind of pain increasingly motivated you as you ventured out into the world of social interactions: rejection. Because we are social creatures and depend on the group for so much of what we value, being rejected (criticized, excluded, teased, bullied, ignored, embarrassed) becomes a very uncomfortable kind of pain that we diligently seek to avoid. Approval is what we seek, and so you sought out people who welcomed you.

Learning how to gain acceptance and avoid rejection is infinitely more complex than learning how to avoid getting burned by a hot pan on the stove. You might be rejected one time for a behavior that was never a problem in the past. Something that was accepted or tolerated by some members of your team may be vigorously disapproved of by your new leader. The same person might be pleased to receive your hug one day and reject it on another for reasons that are completely invisible to you.

This is where the value of social and emotional intelligence starts to become much more apparent. This set of learned skills will help you gracefully navigate your way to acceptance by the wide variety of people in the diverse situations that affect your team. Using these skills together will motivate team members to accomplish the same goals.

A research team at the University of California in Los Angeles discovered a physiological basis for social pain in the area of the mammalian brain called the anterior cingulate cortex (Eisenberger, Lieberman, and Williams, 2003). This area of the brain is activated during both physical pain and the distress caused by social exclusion. The theory is that our social attachment mechanisms associate social exclusion with physical pain to prevent us from separating too much from our social group. This is the first hard evidence that the body automatically processes being excluded by others as a danger on par with physical injury. It demonstrates how deep-seated our need for social connection and inclusion is. Insuring that this need *can be met* for every member of the team is crucial. If your team is so prejudiced against one member, or an individual simply cannot or will not meet the needs and expectations of the team, your team will never fully gel and achieve its full potential.

THE PAIN OF CHANGE

Whether you realize it or not, most of your team members are constantly seeking to apply their cognitive and emotional intelligence to solve the problems that are the work and purpose of your team *while they avoid having to change*.

Rock and Schwartz (2006) note that part of your brain's "hard drive" is allocated to what is called the working memory, where you compare and contrast new information with what you have already stored. Another part of your neural circuitry, in the basal ganglia, is allocated for routine processing of familiar types of information. It forms and holds your long-standing habits, and as long as it is engaged in routine activity, it requires no conscious thought. On the other hand, working memory requires high levels of metabolic energy, so the prefrontal cortex can get your conscious attention.

Much of the day-to-day kinds of work and problem solving we do on the job is routine. Especially when a team has been tackling the same kinds of projects for a while, its members become accustomed to certain patterns of behavior that develop a momentum of their own. When confronted with new challenges, everyone is required to reallocate the distribution of energy in their brain. The energy must be shifted from the basal ganglia and directed to the prefrontal cortex, where it can be used to figure out how the new situation differs from the old one and consequently, what sorts of changes in strategy will be required. This demands a level of attention and extra effort that generally feels uncomfortable and becomes increasingly taxing to produce and sustain over long periods of time. That's why they call it work!

In a similar manner, the brain learns to recognize familiar sensory patterns in the environment, and with repeated observation it expects them to be present as a stable feature of reality. When the brain experiences a disparity between what it expects and what is actually happening, it has a tiny tantrum and emits strong signals that radiate high levels of energy. These signals are generated in the part of the brain called the orbital frontal cortex, and activating it draws energy away from the prefrontal region. Because the orbital frontal cortex is located close to the amygdala, which is the brain's fear management center, the energy necessary for the executive functions of the prefrontal cortex can get detoured into the service of regressive fear-based behavior.

For your team to establish the sustainable changes necessary to solve new challenges, it needs the motivation to develop new levels of both cognitive and emotional intelligence. Discovering new information requires knowing where to look and how to recognize it, but in many ways, that is the easier task to accomplish. The roll-up-your-sleeves hard part is getting your individual team members highly motivated so that they can interrupt established energy allocation routes and establish new patterns, in spite of the fact that it hurts! Rewiring isn't for the faint of heart. To coordinate this level of team motivation, all seven ingredients may need to be employed, sometimes with dogged determination.

TIPS FOR GROWING YOUR TEAM'S MOTIVATIONAL SKILLS

- Set up a central bulletin board or whiteboard, a place where you can display a large poster or colored drawing of the images and words that make up your current most important goal. If possible, include inspirational reasons for reaching the goal— for example, if you meet your numbers, the boss will give you that promised bonus.
- The most powerful motivator can often be to model the kinds of behaviors that you personally think are most important for the team. Let's say there's a lot of procrastination, so you get your work in to everyone not just on time but even a little bit early. Then you might ask each person individually, "Was it helpful to get this before it was actually due?" We assume you will receive agreement. Next time the whole team meets together, make a comment such as "I know we've had some problems in the past getting things to each other on time, so I've been trying to make sure you get all my work early. Is that proving helpful?" There are always exceptions, but we imagine that this would probably be a good example for which everyone would feel grateful. Then as part of the accountability piece, you can simply say something like "I'll do my best to keep this up, and perhaps it will get the ball rolling for the whole team." This needs to be done with an attitude of genuine helpfulness.
- Ask people what they need to make their team experience more productive and more satisfying. Ask them individually once a week or so. In a team meeting, tell people what your own needs are, and then invite them to share. The more

clearly everyone understands what each team member is up against and the needs you are seeking to meet, the easier it is to bridge the gaps. Commit to helping one another meet the reasonable needs that you all come up against.

- Develop a team project prize—dinner at a nice restaurant, a day of skiing or golf, something that everyone can participate in, look forward to, and enjoy. Have a team bank that every member contributes to once a week to publicly show their commitment in any amount up to, say, $20 (not so much that it would be a burden for someone if funds are currently tight). Enjoy the treat when you've reached your goal.

CHAPTER FIVE

THE THIRD SKILL: EMOTIONAL AWARENESS

It ain't what you don't know that gets you into trouble. It's what you know for sure that just ain't so.
MARK TWAIN

It was December 23. We were in the office, and the phone rang. Nobody calls consultants on December 23! It was Elaine, the director of an environmental team in a federal agency, and she was not brimming with holiday cheer. In fact, she was at the end of her rope. She was planning to take a vacation over the holiday and enjoy some much deserved time with her family and friends, but she was so upset and bewildered by the upheaval on her team, she was pondering whether to make that vacation permanent. This from a woman who ran a very successful team and had been promoted a few years back!

What had suddenly changed? The agency had hired a new team member, and almost overnight, the team was spiraling downward in a hurry. Innuendo, rumor, and gossip seemed to be everywhere. People began to complain about Elaine. In fact, a mob mentality took over, and the team stormed in to see Elaine's boss without ever going to Elaine first. Elaine was undone. She'd never been so angry or hurt in her entire career.

After much conversation, we were able to help Elaine gain some perspective and a plan. She took her vacation, and when she came back, so did we. We worked with her and the entire team, using an intervention process to deconstruct the team dynamics and help everyone become more emotionally aware and skilled.

We were able to help the team members identify, understand, and correct the negative cycle that now governed their interactions. The addition of a new team member had upset the balance of the team. One longtime team member had never gotten over the fact that Elaine got the promotion that the other member had wanted. This festering wound was reopened when the new team member was added. The new member's penchant for questioning everything and insinuating wrongdoing stirred up uneasiness, discontent, and indirect whining.

The team needed to get back to sound emotional and social fundamentals. The core of the work was building more effective awareness and communication patterns. After a few months of hard work, the team righted itself. The director weathered the challenge well and was able to move her team to a new level of emotional and social intelligence. Performance jumped. And the improvement didn't go unnoticed. Elaine has been given greater responsibilities, and her team is thriving.

The challenging dynamics that plagued her team could have been that team's unraveling; instead, they used the opportunity for personal and team growth, which resulted in tremendous gains for the team and the organization.

What Emotional Awareness Is for Teams

The ESI question is how to meet emotional challenges in a way that strengthens the team's capabilities. Effective awareness is an essential part of the answer. That's so at the personal level and even more so at the team level.

A team's core reason for existing is to identify and solve problems, regardless of whether they are labeled challenges, projects, or opportunities. Solving problems requires good data, and emotions provide a rich resource of data. If you don't think there is any return on investment (ROI) in understanding emotions, you're missing out—in fact, you're leaving money on the table. Understanding emotions and increasing emotional awareness improve performance, which drives results.

Teams learn a great deal when they understand the behaviors that led to an emotional response from one or more of its members. Emotions also reveal much that may be unspoken, and understanding the nonverbal communication will enhance decision making. This is how to build collaborative intelligence. As we defined collaborative intelligence in the Introduction, this high-level engagement is based on synergy flowing from one team member to another. The flow depends on the ability to read one another, a core aspect of empathy. When team members respectfully respond to an emotional response from one of the team members, that person feels understood. Ultimately, people want to be understood more than just about anything else, and receiving that satisfaction generates a positive feeling, which opens the thinking processes. Open thinking allows for a more complete evaluation of the data, improved consideration of alternatives, and overall better problem resolution.

THE SIX INGREDIENTS OF EMOTIONAL AWARENESS FOR TEAMS

Emotional awareness at the individual level is understanding how we feel and why. It also includes communicating those feelings to others. Each of these elements of knowing and communicating can be complex. You may feel upset but not really know why; if someone asked you, you might say you're "just down, that's all." That wouldn't be very helpful to either of you, yet it might be all you know—or it might be all you are willing to risk sharing. Expanding the ability to recognize how you feel and to know what is triggering a particular response is at the heart of much of psychotherapy and of the personal growth movement. After all, growing into being all that you can be requires good data, and understanding your own emotions is a fundamental part of that information. But functioning as a team doesn't require psychotherapy . . . or does it?

When we take emotional awareness to the team level, the awareness and responsiveness needed grow considerably. Not only do you need to exercise your own self-awareness by knowing how you feel, why you feel that way, and then being able to tell others, but you also need to be willing and able to understand and respond well to the emotional information others provide. Depending on your personality, that can be a daunting prospect. Teams exercising a high level of emotional awareness have members who intuit each other's emotions and understand why they feel that way when it's relevant to the team engagement. More important, they know how to respond appropriately. As we investigate what is required for team emotional awareness, we will consider these six ingredients:

1. *Exploring and using information.* Whether someone is excited, nervous, agitated, mildly curious, or outraged provides significant information that needs your consideration. When team members know how to explore and determine what is important, they can balance competing interests.

2. *Comfort with emotions.* Your childhood and lifelong lessons about emotions have a big impact on your ability to notice and respond to others' emotions, but you're not a hostage of your upbringing. The emotionally intelligent team player must move beyond familiar limits and work toward a higher degree of comfort with emotions. If you had the good fortune to grow up with people who were comfortable with their emotions, then having a conversation with colleagues about feelings might be easy for you. If you were taught from a young age that "feelings belong at home," you're likely to prefer clamming up rather than speaking up. However, your childhood need not be your destiny. As you come to appreciate the importance of building emotional resonance within the team, you will feel more comfortable speaking up.

3. *Awareness of a rich assortment of emotional behaviors.* Perceiving emotions and knowing how to respond to them is greatly enhanced by drawing on experience. Fortunately, not all of that experience has to be personally gained. Artistic expression is rich with experience. A profoundly moving film or play, a well-written novel, or a sublimely choreographed dance can give you the experience of bearing witness to and sharing deeply authentic emotion. You can observe and get a measure of experience with the real risks of emotional vulnerability—but here's the catch: you'll learn from other people's experiences only if you risk becoming appropriately vulnerable yourself. You must pay attention and be fully present. Going through life on cruise control won't increase your depth or wisdom.

Emotional awareness can be developed in your teams only if the right atmosphere is established, one that invites respectful listening and reflects interest in knowing more. Teams that don't take time to talk and ask questions often become stale and lose productivity. The vibrancy of being a healthy, growing, self-reflective, and self-correcting system will be missing.

4. *Discerning the gradations.* Emotions have an amazingly broad range. There's a world of difference between agitation and outrage, optimism and gleeful excitement. Members of ESI teams support one another in understanding and responding to emotions. Furthermore, they give those emotional details appropriate weight by asking themselves or one another, "Just how (happy, angry, depressed, . . .) is my colleague?"

5. *Objectivity.* Research has shown that your own emotional state affects your ability to perceive that of others. If one team member is feeling angry, that anger will cloud his or her ability to accurately perceive the emotional state of other team members. Your emotional and perceptual lenses control the crayon box—will you color in a rosy possibility of success on the project or abandon it to be a dull gray?

How can teams authentically express their difficult emotions? Sometimes it may seem that being human and being a good team member are diametrically opposed. When a colleague exasperates you beyond measure, how can that be expressed without wringing the person's neck? The first step is to be aware of your own feelings—awareness allows you to manage your emotions so that they don't own you. The next step might be to do something physical like take a walk or get a drink of water to diffuse the intensity of the energy without negating the real emotion you feel. Managing your emotions is a bit like managing stress. Once you've calmed down, you are more likely to have an effective response.

6. *Graceful responses.* In the ranching country where Marcia grew up, a constructive response to challenging emotions would be something like "Boy, howdy, that's hard!" It was a simple acknowledgment of the complexity of the situation. Yes, it is often a challenge to respond gracefully to the emotions

of others. That's why we have an entire chapter on enhancing communication skills that can assist you in making an empathic response that is graceful and compelling.

Tim and Sally are in their weekly team meeting, and Sally's enthusiasm is driving Tim crazy. If Tim wants to get Sally to be more realistic from his perspective, he'll be most successful if Sally feels like he understands her enthusiasm even if he doesn't agree with it. He'll accomplish that goal only if he responds to her with respect. That means acknowledging her before he gives his alternative perspective. So it's not "Sally, you always want to change things. Now be realistic for once" but rather "Sally, you really care about this. It's great to see your enthusiasm, but I'm concerned about the impact to our team's success if we don't finish the other projects first." This ingredient calls for us to have empathy for our teammates and for them to experience that empathy.

WHY TEAMS NEED EMOTIONAL AWARENESS

"You're rushing this for the sake of a profit, and you just don't care!" Patti hissed, glaring in dismay at a half-dozen men and women in well-tailored suits. "The bottom line isn't all this is about; what about the people who live here, who call this home?" Patti's anger was so deep she trembled. While she loved the old building in which they stood, she loved the people who lived there more— hardworking, low-income folks who were about to be displaced so that new, upscale condos could be built, kindling a "neighborhood renaissance." This was no renaissance. This was a takeover.

Kelly, the president of the neighborhood organization, looked at his friend and fellow board member. This was getting extreme, and he wasn't sure what to do.

Fortunately, Danielle spoke up to comfort Patti. "This is hard for you Patti; I see the distress on your face. I so wish this wasn't happening; you know how hard it is on our neighborhood board," Danielle said forlornly.

"This isn't about us," Patti seethed. "It's about the people being displaced. It's about the beauty of the park being compromised when they tear down this lovely old building and put up a twenty-story high-rise. This is tragic."

RJ, the city councilwoman from the neighborhood, was tapping her foot, getting increasingly impatient. "Look, there's no backtracking; this is a done deal. The neighborhood association gets a stipend for your work in helping distribute the antiques and cultural memorabilia from the building, and the developers, according to their legal rights, will tear down the building and begin construction." She breathed a frustrated sigh.

Deon and Aisha, also representatives from the neighborhood board, were just looking back and forth as this drama unfolded. But then Aisha said, "Look, there's a lot of emotion here today. It's on all of our faces; I hear it in our voices, and we can all feel the tension is at a fevered pitch. We all care about being good neighbors. Let's not forget that. We'll be here a long time, and the people who buy these condos will love the park and probably belong to the neighborhood organization. We can't undo the deal, but we can choose how we deal with the deal. We can still do a lot. We still have a choice in how we move forward with things. Let's look at small steps."

Patti looked at her with a mixture of interest, skepticism, and rage.

Aisha's husband, Deon, jumped in with an idea. "What if we help find new homes for the people who need to move? I know it's not the same, but since they are moving, we can show them that they really matter by doing something tangible. Since Aisha and I run an apartment building a few blocks from here, we have a lot of connections with people who are renting places all over town. We may even be able to find some units next to each other so neighbors could move into the same building."

Patti moved a little closer and grudgingly flipped to a fresh page on her tablet and pulled out a pen. She gave a quick nod. "Let's get to it."

How the Team Applied the Six Ingredients

Patti was experiencing several emotions, and they were escalating. She couldn't get out of the grief and anger she was feeling on her own. Her friend Danielle helped by acknowledging her distress, though she missed the depth of distress Patti was experiencing.

Danielle demonstrated comfort with emotions. RJ's impatience and the affirmation that the deal wasn't negotiable actually provided information that Deon and Aisha used constructively. Aisha began to turn an ugly situation into a positive process in her gentle challenge to Patti. She recognized that the level of distress Patti was feeling was escalating, and she was skillfully able to halt it by tapping into Patti's commitment to the neighborhood. Aisha deftly refocused Patti on solutions, on looking for what could be done. She was able to connect with Patti just enough to decelerate the emotion.

Aisha's response opened the door for Deon's brainstorm. The soft one-two way Deon and Aisha worked together to diffuse the situation, while respecting Patti's agony, created a graceful and practical way to turn around the energy and the outcome.

EXPOSING THE PROCESS OF EMOTIONAL AWARENESS

What enables you to become emotionally aware? It's actually a seven-step process that can transpire in the blink of an eye or in a protracted succession. Emotional awareness is the result of this sequence:

1. Sense the emotion (feeling).
2. Acknowledge the feeling.
3. Identify more facts.
4. Accept the feeling.
5. Reflect on why that emotion is showing up in that moment. Notice what other feelings are present or came before it. Ask yourself what its purpose might be, what it is communicating, demonstrating, or trying to teach you.
6. Act—bring your thoughts and feelings up at the team meeting or with someone individually, and take appropriate action, if needed.
7. Reflect on the usefulness of the response and what lesson you would like to take away.

Perhaps surprisingly, the next thing you know, you'll be right back at the beginning of the sequence, because all aspects of life, including business, are packed with emotion. You'll find that you just keep looping through the sequence. It's rather like the diagram shown in Figure 5.1.

Emotional Contagion

Sigal Barsade (2002), of the Wharton School at the University of Pennsylvania, is a leading researcher on the effect of emotions on groups. Her article "The Ripple Effect: Emotional Contagion and

Figure 5.1. The Circle of Emotion.

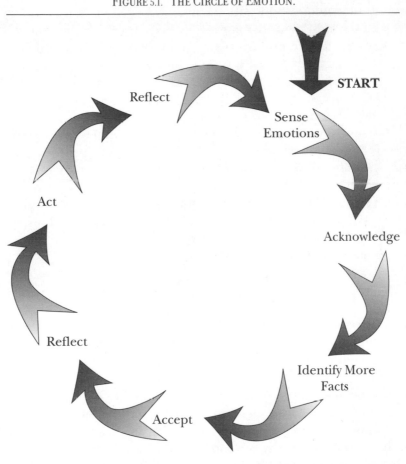

Its Influence on Group Behavior" provides important documentation that people are "walking mood inductors" and that those influences can make an organizationwide impact. Emotional contagion is a great description of how emotions are shared even when it's unintentional.

Barsade finds that these shared social processes may occur in two ways. The first is through a spontaneous, unconscious process based on the innate human tendency to mimic the behavior of others. For instance, research shows that people automatically mimic each other's facial expressions. This mimicking is largely communicated through nonverbal behaviors including tonality. The amount of attention we give one another has a big impact on how much emotion we'll pick up.

The second is a more cognitive process in which the recipient of someone else's emotions uses that emotion as "social information to understand how he or she should be feeling" (Barsade, 2002, p. 648). When you witness a trusted colleague having an angry response to news about a restructuring of your department, that may influence you to react angrily as well.

Barsade's conclusion is that "group members experience moods at work, these moods ripple out and, in the process, influence not only other group members' emotions but their group dynamics and individual cognitions, attitudes, and behaviors as well. Thus, emotional contagion, through its direct and indirect influence on employees' and work teams' emotions, judgments, and behaviors, can lead to subtle but important ripple effects in groups and organizations" (2002, p. 670).

SOCIAL AWARENESS

To heighten the understanding of social awareness, Daniel Goleman's definition of the topic provides a useful context in demonstrating the breadth of this concept. He writes that it "refers to a spectrum that runs from instantaneously *sensing* another's inner state, to *understanding* her feelings and thoughts, to '*getting*' complicated social situations" (2006, p. 84).

Think of the many social contexts in which emotional information shared within your team is influential. For example, the expression of empathy first requires being aware of someone's emotions and the circumstances that gave rise to them. Noticing when someone becomes frustrated and responding can prevent an angry outburst. A high degree of emotional awareness is intrinsically linked to developing political savvy. Every successful politician, CEO, diplomat, and leader uses emotional awareness to understand the dynamics in play and design appropriate strategies for the situation. The strength of your political savvy is based on the quality of your social and emotional awareness, on how well you read the environment, the people, and the messages being sent. It is also crucial to keep in mind that some people will strategically misrepresent their emotional responses or attempt to manipulate those of others in order to affect the outcome of the decision-making process. Stay aware.

USING YOUR REFLECTIVE SKILLS

There should be a monument to the opposable thumb, since most of what has been built in the physical world over the ages wouldn't have been possible without that diminutive digit. At the personal and interpersonal levels, the ability to reflect on our actions, thoughts, and choices is a similarly important attribute, and no doubt it deserves a monument of its own! Unfortunately, we haven't learned to use this skill nearly as well yet. There's a direct correlation between emotional and social intelligence and using our reflective skills. The better we use our reflective capacity, the higher some aspects of our ESI will be.

The highest levels of emotional intelligence demonstrate spontaneous right action, the natural responsiveness to other people and situations in which our behavior perfectly and with effortless elegance matches what is called for. On these remarkable occasions, our ESI skills are functioning with unconscious competency.

You put your reflective awareness in high gear when you're paying close attention to what you're doing and why. It's a part of the evaluation process after a meeting, a project, an event, or a process. It's the thoughtful deconstruction and analysis of what worked and what didn't. It's why we ask every team member to reflect on the day at the end of a team-building session. Einstein said that insanity is doing the same thing over and over and expecting different results. Introspection is the antidote to that insanity. It can help prevent you from making the same mistake twice.

Allan Hobson describes the development of consciousness as evolving to the adult level when we become "aware of our awareness" (2000, p. 97). This happens with "the gradual building up of symbol upon symbol as brain circuit is added to brain circuit" (p. 80). Well-known authorities on brain functioning, such as Candace Pert, teach that seeing isn't believing, but believing is seeing. One of the best ways to become aware of what's important to other team members is to train yourself to notice finer and finer distinctions in their behavior. Awareness is one of the best tools for breaking out of your own hypnotic trance and seeing the rest of the world in fresh ways. Of course, any asset can be used to such extremes that it becomes a detriment. In *Blink*, Malcolm Gladwell (2005) warns us not to overanalyze, as it can erase right-brain intuitive benefits. Balance is the trick!

To design effective ESI exercises for teams, coaches, and leaders, we always ask our clients to reflect. We're likely to include directions such as "Briefly describe how each team member responded when your team competed in that game and why." This is pivotal to expanding the ESI skills of each team member and of the team as a whole. It takes conscious awareness to recognize what works and to refine the rest to improve an outcome. We are not suggesting that being aware will suddenly result in the creation of new skills. New skills are mastered through repeated practice, which gives new neurons the opportunity to fire often enough to physiologically build the circuitry that supports the new behavior. Both are required—awareness and action.

STRATEGIES FOR TEAM AWARENESS

The process of reflection is also called mindfulness, awareness, or introspection. Suzette Bryan (2006) describes one way of developing this skill through her "imagined interaction theory," which calls for imagining or rehearsing a conversation with specificity before it happens or reflecting on one that is completed. This technique is one of many ways of using conscious awareness to enhance a team's emotional intelligence. Imagine the organization meeting where your team is making a key presentation. As a team, imagine the presentation. Rehearse and reflect on the presentation. Hear the success—all the congratulations. Bryan suggests that the process calls for imaging both verbal and nonverbal behaviors. What do you see as you imagine the presentation: nodding, smiles, quizzical looks? This is critical, as so much of our actual communication is nonverbal. It is one of the primary techniques professional athletes have used successfully for decades.

Richard Boyatzis and Annie McKee (2005) focus on the application of mindfulness, hope, and compassion in their book *Resonant Leadership*. Many of their numerous strategies can be used to support effective teams as well as leaders.

Take a moment to think of an important discussion with one of your team members. Imagine in detail what might occur or did occur. Now imagine constructive changes to that conversation. Make the changes specific—alter your tonality, adjust your posture, change the words. Noticing what works can make team members and the whole team much more successful. Here's another idea: create mental movies. This can be a creative strategy to suggest if your team gets stuck on a tough subject. Set aside a few minutes, invite team members to form pairs, and have them brainstorm some alternative realities and then share the results with one another. The team has fun, the tension dissipates, and you may well find that a creative solution pops up.

Think of the teams you work with and the strategies the team uses to reflect. If your team doesn't have processes for reflecting and evaluating, it needs to experiment and find a few. There are many possibilities. For example, the whole team might meet to evaluate the process of conducting a project and to consider its success. Real conscious awareness at the team level happens when a team takes time to discuss how well its strategies and tactics actually worked. Did you listen to one another? Was there enough flexibility to take time to consider alternatives, to celebrate intermediate successes along the way, to build fun and camaraderie into the process? Often teams forget to consider this component; instead they are caught up with external facts such as whether the project was on time, whether ROI was on track, if the budget was met, if the boss was impressed, or whether constituents are happy with the outcome.

The immediate external success of a project often gets an undue percentage of the attention, resulting in an exclusive focus on short-term results. This can result in strategic blunders and missed opportunities from not evaluating the long-term impacts on the team. If team members are happy and feel noticed and rewarded for their work, they will hang in with the project longer, will be more resourceful if they need to work long hours, and will be healthier. This is all a part of positive psychology, which will be discussed more thoroughly in Chapter Nine on positive mood.

You may also conduct much of your reflecting informally with individuals or smaller groupings of your team. In essence, it's the "water cooler moment." You go to get a glass of water, meet a colleague, and say, "How are you feeling about the tension in our team meetings? This constant focus on deadlines is eating up our creativity." The discussion is engaged. Take it seriously when you and your teammates take time to consider how things are going. Note and value the depth of discussion. Act on your recognitions; this is valid feedback, and it reinforces active awareness.

WHOLE-MIND PERCEIVING

Neurons are the "thinking cells" of our body, and they are spread from head to toe. We have more neurons in our gut than in our brain, and there are so many neurons around the heart that the HeartMath Institute refers to it as a second brain. That's the origin of our concept of "team HBG (heart-brain-gut) thinking"; it's a nutty world, and we need our best thinking to thrive in it. That means our wisdom should come from all three places: heart, brain, and gut. There are several popular ways to refer to this integration, such as combining rational and intuitive thinking or right- and left-brain thinking. It takes real discipline to develop the skill to access these different forms of being smart. Some authors in the field of neuroscience have begun referring to body and mind as a single unit in much the same way as physicists use the expression *space-time continuum*. The title of Pert's (2004) audio presentation, *Your Body Is Your Subconscious Mind*, shows just how deeply the two are integrated.

Some of us are analytical thinkers—we love to get the data, study them, do more research, and really know the technical aspects of what we're talking about before we make a decision. This is critical in many circumstances. No one wants a nuclear-fired power plant operated without considerable thought and state-of-the-art research. Yet there are times when that much analysis will stymie a team's progress, making it seem like it's operating in slow motion or trying to talk underwater. The activity is so distorted that understanding and appreciation are lost. This is paralysis by analysis—something you've probably experienced once or twice. A strong team knows how to balance its thinking styles—at times analytical, at other times spontaneous and intuitive.

The alternative to analysis is described well in *Blink* when Gladwell talks about the value of snap decisions. He shows by example how quickly accurate decisions can be made. People trained in observing couples in conflict can predict with a high degree of accuracy whether a marriage will last, based on an amazingly small amount of data. Depending on the degree of training, they can be 90 percent accurate when observing for fifteen minutes and nearly as accurate in only three minutes. Psychologists Nalini Ambady and Robert Rosenthal (1993) found that if they showed students a video of six to fifteen seconds of a teacher's presentation, they could rate the teacher's effectiveness, and there would be a high degree of correlation with the end-of-semester evaluations. Fifteen minutes? Fifteen seconds? Yikes! Just how are these snap decisions made, and when should we trust them? Gladwell (2005, p. 23) explains that this happens due to "thin slicing," which "refers to the ability of our unconscious to find patterns in situations and behavior based on very narrow slices of experience." It results from rapid cognition, taking a quick look and recognizing the patterns at an unconscious level.

When should a team follow its members' thin-slicing capabilities, and when should they take more time to explore alternatives, gather facts, and deliberate? There's no simple answer. In large part, the decision should be based on a combination of the experience within the team. Does the person who just made the snap decision have credibility? Is there a foundation of prior experiences and training that informs that quick decision? The team leader and members with influence will hold considerable sway on whether to accept the quick decision. The best process calls for integrating the rational and intuitive thinking powers of team awareness to guide the choice, and this needs to be done with attention to the emotions stirred up.

Will all the team members be able to go with the quick decision even though they don't understand why it's the right one? If not, it can be worthwhile, even mission-critical, to give them enough processing time to reach the conclusion themselves. We've been brought in to work on many a conflict that arises from part of a team's being pushed into a decision the members are just not ready to embrace. Often a bit of patience leads to a big payoff. Achieving the balance calls for a direct application of the team's emotional awareness.

If Roberto's feeling agitated and deeply suspicious that the new way won't work and Eunice is impatient because she's certain she knows the way to go based on her past experience and intuition, how do the two of them and the team get on the same page? The answer depends on the dynamics of the situation, but in general, we recommend · noting the differences and validating that both views are understandable. We call for patience, balanced by a commitment to move forward promptly. We then suggest that someone on the team ask Roberto what else he needs. That information will help Eunice and other members who agree with her approach work with Roberto and others who may need more answers or more processing time. The team members should call a huddle and do some reality checking together. For example, we might suggest to the team, imagine you go with Eunice's idea and it's six months later. Let your intuition guide you in exploring whether it is working or not. Cast these future conditions for durability and workability in your imagination. What else do you need to know? These and similar questions can help the team use the wisdom of both members and get everyone on board while moving forward at a reasonable pace.

INTROVERTS AND EXTROVERTS: ENGAGING AND AVOIDING THE TEAM DANCE

What do Warren Buffet, Bill Gates, Steven Spielberg, and Sara Lee CEO Brenda Barnes have in common? According to a *USA Today* column (Jones, 2006), they are CEOs or leaders, and they are all introverts. Many of us think that a good CEO will be charismatic, outgoing, and sociable, yet results from the Myers-Briggs Type Indicator reveal that 39 percent of male corporate leaders and 34 percent of female corporate leaders are introverts.

One's tendency toward being an introvert or an extrovert affects the team, its identity, and its ability to work with emotions effectively. Both tendencies can bring strengths and weaknesses to the team dance. Powerful teams are aware of these tugs and pulls and know how to use them well. In general, extroverts are more likely to be comfortable talking about emotions; introverts, less so. Extroverts often process information by talking, thereby occasionally saying something regrettable as they work their way toward a decision. Introverts may tend to leave a concern unaddressed in order to keep the peace, but often that results in an exploding problem that could have been nipped in the bud. Extroverts may move too fast in their discussions and decision making, leaving introverts feeling bruised, ready to retreat, or ignored. These situations can be averted with awareness. Each team member benefits from understanding his or her own tendencies and those of others. This can add the rational grounding needed to help the fast-moving person be more patient or give the more deliberate person the extra encouragement needed to take the risk and move forward.

TIPS FOR GROWING YOUR TEAM'S EMOTIONAL AWARENESS

> *Being empathic is a complex, demanding, and strong—yet also a subtle and gentle—way of being.*
> CARL ROGERS

Examples of strategies for building your team's emotional awareness have been sprinkled throughout this chapter. You can also go to resources such as our book *Emotional Intelligence in Action* (Hughes, Patterson, and Terrell, 2005) for strategies to grow a team's competencies. An open, curious attitude will strongly support a team's ability to grow its ESI skills. With that in mind, try any of these:

- *Develop the team's emotional vocabulary.* Put a list on the wall in your meeting area, and add new words as they are recognized.

The leader can give a dollar to anyone who comes up with new words to add to the vocabulary. Perhaps in the spirit of building camaraderie, the one who gets the most money will share the winnings by buying treats for the next team meeting. Ice cream anyone?

- *Practice empathy and empathic communication.* Empathy is the capacity for experiencing awareness and caring for another's feelings, volitions, or ideas. A strict, unfeeling statement to a team member is likely to create defensiveness and hostility rather than create a connection. Responding with empathy means that the team member will act or speak in a way that demonstrates respect, understanding, and patience (agreement is not required). It requires moving at a pace that will be experienced as respectful by the receiver.

There are many ways to enhance this skill for the team. First, direct training and practice with empathy provide a valuable foundation. Then the team members can agree to operate with empathy and catch one another doing it right. What gets noticed gets repeated, so noticing the behaviors you do want is valuable. If there is a breach of empathy, point it out to the person who made the mistake. That might mean a discrete talk in private first and then finding a more general way to discuss the lesson in front of the whole team.

- *Increase familiarity and trust among teammates.* Build in deliberate ways for team members to get to know one another and to develop trust in those relationships. Pair up the members of the team once a week or once every other week, with an expectation that they will go to lunch, share strategies on work matters, and tell one another more about themselves. Keep shifting pairs so that you continue the team building. People might object that this shouldn't be structured, that lunches should happen naturally. Sometimes structure is good. It certainly need not determine the content of the conversation, and the occasional deadline can be a motivator. Check out how much time the team members are spending with one another one on one and whether this communication is balanced around the table. If so, great; the strategy isn't needed.

We'll bet that given how busy most folks are, the team could greatly benefit from the structure. Marcia has a great example of this benefit. She and her friend Caroline met the first day they each began practicing law. Both clerked for judges on the 10th Circuit Court of Appeals. Lawyers with families have trouble making deep friendships—there just isn't time. Recognizing this, they decided to buy season tickets to the local theater every year. The tickets were a tool to get them together several times a year. It's worked marvelously for decades. And as their relationship evolved, they discovered they are actually distant cousins!

- *Learn to speak up and to listen.* The introvert may need to practice speaking up more, and the extrovert may need to practice listening more. However it works, a team thrives because of the application of both of these skills. You could develop an intention that you'll hear from everyone at least once in a meeting to encourage balanced dialogue and speaking up. During our team sessions, many introverts tell their fellow teammates that it is very hard to get a word in edgewise. Don't wait for your leader to invite their contribution; remind one another periodically of the value of listening and practice it with intention. Notice how great both the listener and the one being listened to end up feeling. Reinforcing those positive feelings helps us keep them growing.

CHAPTER SIX

THE FOURTH SKILL: COMMUNICATION

*Who you are speaks so loudly I can't hear
what you're saying.*
RALPH WALDO EMERSON

The reputation of the IT department in a midsize manufacturing company had gone from unremarkable to nearly irreparable. The staff were tagged as unresponsive, aloof, and asleep at the wheel. The good news was that their technical competencies weren't questioned. Paula, the HR director for the company, called, asking us how such highly qualified, brilliant personnel could have developed such a terrible group reputation. It was absolutely bewildering.

The first challenge was comparatively easy to address. The public face of the IT department belonged to the technicians who went to employees' workstations to do on-site repairs. These folks were highly introverted. They were also pretty smart. They figured out when to show up to do the repairs when the employees were least likely to be at their desks. That way, they wouldn't need to talk with employees they didn't know. They slipped in at lunchtime. They paid attention to departmental schedules and stopped by when the team was in a meeting or they made e-mail inquiries about schedules. Employees thought they were trying to schedule a repair time when the employee would be there, but actually, the opposite was true!

This system worked great for the technicians but seriously frustrated the employees. Repairs were always made in a timely manner, but employees had no idea that the technician had come and gone, so they had no reason to believe that the problem had been fixed. This was easily remedied by creating "calling cards" that the technicians signed and left when they finished repairs. The card read, "Hi, I worked on your computer, and the problem is fixed. Please call if you have any more problems. Thanks."

This simple fix helped, but it wasn't enough. We then worked with the IT team members to improve their verbal communication skills and their comfort with speaking up. It was a slow, respectful process that enhanced skills and behaviors so that their introversion wouldn't be an impediment to their success or their reputation. We started by having them work on greeting people that they passed in the halls or saw in the cafeteria. This took a lot of practice, but it helped the whole team. As they got more comfortable, they realized that they felt more respected, more a part of the organization, and that they were actually happier.

We also helped them increase their internal communication skills. Over time, they were able to make active discussions a routine part of their team meetings. The results have been outstanding. The reputation of the IT department has not just been restored but actually enhanced, and the team itself functions at a whole new level.

Communication is the lifeblood of all teamwork. Its essential ingredients include all the technical aspects, such as senders and receivers, messages, filters, and signs and signals, but our simple and perhaps most useful definition of communication arises out of the real purpose it is meant to fulfill.

Communication is what people do to connect with others so that they can satisfy their needs and desires to make life better.

THE SIX INGREDIENTS OF TEAM COMMUNICATION

1. *Sender.* The sender is the person who needs to communicate—give info, ask for assistance, provide feedback, get recognition, or make a request. In short, the sender needs something from somebody and is seeking to get that need addressed.

2. *Receiver.* The receiver is the person that the sender wants to influence. If the sender is successful in his or her attempts to communicate, it will change the receiver's behavior in some manner.

3. *Message.* The message is the package of information that is transferred from the sender to the receiver. Technically, information is defined as "the reduction of uncertainty." Thus the message expands the receiver's knowledge and awareness of the environment by reducing uncertainty about the specific situation.

4. *Meaning.* While the complete meaning of the communication is never limited to the words exclusively, this term generally refers to the verbal content of the communication. This includes the letters and words that make up the symbolic language used to represent objects and actions in the real world. These symbols convey the rational content of the message. The complete meaning of the message, including the nonverbal components, can only be conveyed once, in real time, whereas the rational or cognitive representation of it can be repeated any number of times.

5. *Feeling.* The feeling of the communication is conveyed primarily through the nonsymbolic content, the dimension that includes such distinctions as tonality, posture, gestures, facial expressions, and eye contact. These convey the feelings or emotional energy behind the message and lets the receiver know if the sender is seeking support or opposition in response.

6. *Technique.* The technique of communication includes attitudes and skills such as respect, listening, matching, building rapport, giving accurate feedback, attending, reflecting, pacing, and leading. This is probably the most complex and significant ingredient in successful communication.

The skillful application of all six ingredients enables the receiver to receive and understand the meaning of the message.

WHY TEAMS NEED GOOD COMMUNICATION

"Ladies and gentleman, may I have your attention please. Flight 484 has been canceled due to mechanical problems; please return to the ticket counter, where our agents will reconfirm your reservation on another flight."

All 186 passengers on the flight from Phoenix to Newark would need to be accommodated on other aircraft. It was 6:15 PM on a Sunday evening, and the airline had only one more flight to Newark that night—a smaller plane that was more than half full.

Allie was supervisor of the ticket counter, and she called a quick huddle before the deluge hit. "OK, everybody, heads up! We've got a bit of a meltdown here, but we've all been through this before, and we'll get through it tonight. This shift has some of the highest customer service ratings for the season, and there's no team I'd rather face this with, so take a deep breath. Good, now take *another* deep breath because it's going to be a long night."

The first thirty-one people were rebooked on the later flight, and forty-eight more got out on the two other carriers who had late-night service, but once there were no more planes leaving Phoenix that night, things started overheating. Sharon's first five or six customers were compliant, but the next one was a real piece of work.

"What's wrong with you, anyway? Why would you work for a company full of morons? Are you a moron too? I'm not going to a hotel; I'm going to Newark tonight! I have to give a presentation to the senior leadership of Citibank first thing tomorrow morning. This is not a deal that's going to wait because your mechanics are morons, so don't lie to me. I know you've got seats blocked off for people like me who have to get there!"

As resilient as ticket agents are, they all have their limits to the amount of tears, pleading, and hostility they can tolerate. Sharon had reached hers and was becoming increasingly hostile herself.

Matthew was next to her on one side, Janine on the other. Matthew drew her aside and said, "Tough crowd tonight. Looks like they're not cutting you any slack either."

"That jerk just called me a moron and a liar," she said.

"Name calling is the worst," he responded. "You must feel pretty offended."

"Offended? Offended? Puhleez! Just leave me alone!" she snapped.

Matthew returned to his customer, smarting from her rebuff.

Sharon's next customer was an elderly lady who couldn't hear very well, and Sharon ended up shouting the instructions for reclaiming the woman's bag. That upset Matthew's next customer, who turned surly and snarled, "What do you expect from a bunch of robots?"

Between customers, Janine escaped to see Allie, who was working frantically at her computer to find additional seats. "Sharon is losing it, Allie," she said. "We've got to get her out of there."

"Are you crazy?" Allie replied. "I can't. You know better than I do how long the line is."

Janine moved closer until she was right up against the desk. She put her hands on her hips and looked Allie directly in the eyes. "Allie, you've got to get her out of there right now, at least for a little while. She's not just upsetting the customers; she's upsetting Matthew and me and who knows how many others!"

Allie pushed back from her desk and stood up. Janine had her full attention now. "OK, Janine, this must be more serious than I thought. After her next customer, tell her to come see me about rebooking passengers on a one-stop through Houston."

Janine returned to her position and gave Sharon the news. Sharon went back to see Allie, who asked nonchalantly, "How's it going out there?"

"Miserable!" Sharon shot back. "They're all a bunch of stupid, impatient jerks."

"Right, they're stupid, impatient jerks, and it looks like they're really getting under your skin." The compassion in Allie's voice was too much.

Sharon broke down weeping. She began crying so hard she couldn't speak. Allie handed her a box of tissues and just stood by quietly until the tears subsided. "You've handled hostile, frustrated passengers a thousand times, and you've never been this upset. This is not about the jerks. What is it, Sharon?" She reached out and touched Sharon's arm.

"My mother was just diagnosed with Alzheimer's," she said quietly.

"I'm so sorry. Please sit down." She gestured. Allie rolled her chair around in front of the desk and sat down too. "I'm so sorry," she repeated.

"I was afraid of this. I just kept hoping maybe she was just forgetting. But more and more of what she says means absolutely nothing," Sharon said, now crying again.

"I'm so sorry," Allie said again gently. After a moment, she continued, "I don't want you to work the counter anymore tonight, Sharon. This is the flight from hell. But we really do need your help if you're up to it. Why don't you work on lost bags—it's pretty quiet down there tonight—and send Shakir up to the counter."

"Oh, OK. Thank you. I'm sorry," Sharon said as she stood up.

Allie rose as well and gave Sharon a warm embrace. "Thank you for staying. We really need your help, but if you think it's going to be too tough, let me know, and I'll send you home."

HOW THE TEAM APPLIED THE SIX INGREDIENTS

These team members have clearly developed their emotional and social intelligence as a team. They are able to assess accurately how other team members feel and how significant those feelings are. That, and their willingness to communicate compassionately and directly with each other, gave this situation as happy an ending as possible. Matthew's first attempt to reflect what Sharon was feeling and why was not successful. It was a very good attempt, but his choice of the word *offended* somehow wasn't accurate—either not quite strong enough or not quite what she was feeling. Maybe she was just too vulnerable to respond.

Janine's intervention with Allie was critical, but she had to use some pretty dramatic nonverbal communication to get Allie's attention. Moving right up against Allie's desk, as close as she could, putting her hands on her hips, calling her by name, and then looking directly in her eyes is a very powerful package of nonverbal communication. In this context, each gesture means only one thing—I want your attention now!

Allie responded very well, first giving Janine and then Sharon her fullest attention. When she realized the nature of the crisis, her verbal and nonverbal behavior was highly effective. Moving a chair around in front of her desk meant, "There's absolutely nothing more important than this to me right now." Her techniques were both compassionate and professional.

Asking Sharon to stay was both in the team's best interest and in Sharon's. In one way, she needed to feel like she belonged more than ever. If her teammates hadn't realized that she was not able to perform competently at that moment, things could have gotten pretty ugly out front at the counter. Sharon's pain might have led her to say things that could have resulted in irreversible harm to the organization's reputation and her own career.

FOUR CONDITIONS FOR EFFECTIVE COMMUNICATION

Communication is a magical dance you do with others to bridge the gap between yourself and your teammates, family members, the rest of the world. What makes communication effective is a vast topic—it's the stuff of wars and legends, the rise and fall of political leaders, corporate successes and failures, inspirational triumphs—and it is the everyday infrastructure that defines our career paths and our most cherished relationships.

Our more formal definition of team communication is "the process of sharing information to meet some need or desire in which one team member sends a message that is received by another team or team member and gets acknowledged." All three steps have to occur for communication to take place. The idea that the information shared in communication is intended to meet some need or desire is perhaps self-evident, but we highlight that to emphasize that the basic intention of communication is positive. Obviously, the results are not always positive, but they are always the result of someone attempting to get their needs or desires met.

The six ingredients of communication combine in a variety of ways to meet the four conditions for effective communication: purpose, form, content, and role.

PURPOSE

The first step in building team communication that is emotionally and socially intelligent is to understand *why* people communicate in the first place. Someone needs more information to help solve a problem.

Sometimes team members may send inaccurate information either by mistake or in an attempt to gain some personal advantage. The quality of the information that a sender relays is significantly influenced by his or her sense of well-being. A higher sense of well-being reduces defensiveness, increases cooperative behavior, and improves the quality of the information sent.

Consider for a moment the various communication patterns of the people on your team. No matter how frustrating or dysfunctional their behavior might appear at first, examining it in this light reveals that there's a method to their madness. If it seems that your teammates are attempting to satisfy their needs at your expense or at the expense of the team, it reflects the level of security they feel and the amount of value they place on belonging to the group. Taking an objective look at team behavior that is unproductive can remove the personal sting that might otherwise become a problem if one or more members feel they have been unfairly treated. For example, a leadership team at a midsize company is developing a strategic plan. To be sure it's implemented, Jose insists that the objectives have specific details, including who is responsible to do what and by when. He continually asks questions to fill in these details as soon as a new idea surfaces. Ernie understands that some specificity should be included, but he's frustrated with the focus on detail at the expense of creative exploration. He seeks to use good communication skills by first acknowledging Jose's concern for developing a practical document that leaves no confusion. Ernie agrees that they don't want confusion, but he invites Jose to join him in finding ways to allow for more creativity. Ernie proposes that they use this session for creative discussion and then develop a separate document at the following meeting to flesh out the details.

FORM

The next step in developing ESI communication within teams is to understand the two basic forms of communication, verbal and nonverbal. Even though we humans are very partial to our verbal language, we give it much more credit than it deserves. The actual words in our messages convey only about 7 percent of the meaning that we share. This is surprisingly small and extremely important to take into account. Sigal Barsade (2002), whose research on emotional contagion we discussed in Chapter Five, cites research by Albert Mehrabian: "In a study of emotional communication, Mehrabian found that when interacting with others, only 7 percent of subjects' emotional understanding of the other person stemmed from the words spoken, [whereas] 38 percent and 55 percent were attributed to verbal tone and facial expression, respectively" (p. 650).

There is tremendous opportunity for misunderstanding if e-mail is used as a primary communication medium, since only 7 percent of meaning comes from the words themselves. It is infinitely more complex to communicate effectively with geographically dispersed team members than for team members in physical proximity. E-mail seems like an attractive communication tool, but beware: the nonverbal portion, 93 percent of the message, is entirely missing. Whenever possible, speak to each other in real time on the phone—that adds 35 percent more meaning to your message.

E-mail is great for communicating the time of a meeting, but if you want to let someone know how you feel about your role in the most important team project of the year, e-mail may be disastrous. Even your local teammates need to read your nonverbal messages to fully understand and respond to your concerns.

Nonverbal communication is extremely powerful because it is modulated unconsciously for both sender and receiver. Bar-On and his coauthors (2003) noted that "it has also been suggested that another fundamental difference between cognitive (IQ) and emotional and social intelligence (ESI) may be that cognitive intelligence is more cortically strategic in nature, while emotional and social intelligence is more limbically tactical for immediate behavior suited more for survival and adaptation" (p. 1792). Verbal symbols better satisfy our conscious cognitive needs, while nonverbal communication addresses our emotional and social needs.

Teams have developed enormous complexity along the trajectory from hunting and gathering to virtual teams spread across the planet. The Internet has radically changed our ability to connect, but it will be interesting to see how adding sound and video to e-mail may eventually restore some nonverbal components to our high-tech communications. The value of this to people who work together on nonlocal teams cannot be overemphasized.

Although the verbal part of communication conveys only 7 percent of the total meaning the receiver derives, it is of ultimate value. The verbal content includes the topic that all our feelings and intentions are focused on, along with the rules for encoding and sequencing the symbols on the shared meaning of which we all rely. This part of communication is accomplished through the most powerful tool ever created by human beings: language. The word *language* derives from the Latin word *lingua,* meaning "tongue." and this extraordinary organ certainly ranks right up there with the opposable thumb for the evolutionary advantages it has given people. But the gift of speech is a two-edged sword because it profoundly shapes our experience of the world without our conscious knowledge.

Language determines what we *can* see and how we see it by virtue of the way it structures our mind from a very early age. When English-speaking parents attempt to teach their child the name for the object at the center of most sporting events, they will say, "This is a ball, Johnny. Say 'ball.'"

A Native American lecturer pointed out how different this was from the spirit in which language was taught in his tribe. The English translation of what his parents said to him under the same circumstances was, "*We call this* a ball, Johnny. Say 'ball.'" This is a subtle but extremely significant difference. In the first case, the English-speaking parents are installing a rule about being, while in the second case, the Native American parents are simply expanding the child's vocabulary.

We are so accustomed to negotiating our relationship with the external world through language that we fail to realize that language is only a way of describing and representing our experience; it is not the experience itself. To say, "Our team is depressed and unmotivated because the company cannot give any bonuses this year" is only a way of speaking. There is no way any language can convey all of the implications and feelings and consequences of the life conditions that that sentence describes.

Often we end up mistaking our symbolic descriptions for the real world they are meant to describe. Count Korzybski

(1879–1950), the founder and director of the Institute of General Semantics, warned, "The map is not the territory." Language can never include the infinitely rich amount of detail, potential, and experience that is present in reality. "Baseball" is just the generic label that refers to the object in the box at the sporting goods store and the thing that the pitcher is about to throw and the whirling blur of matter coming toward you at eighty miles an hour in the batter's box, but none of them are by any stretch the same thing in reality. Confusing the map with the territory is like going out to a nice restaurant and eating the menu instead of the meal.

CONTENT

The third component in developing ESI communications in teams is to understand the two types of content that the form conveys—meaning and feeling. It's necessary to use words correctly to get the cognitive meaning right, but how do words actually make meaning happen? Words have conventional meanings that are described in dictionaries, but as useful as dictionaries are in listing ways words have been used in the past, the real meanings are always specific to the person who is speaking. If you have any doubt whatsoever about what a word or concept means to the speaker of that word or concept, you had better ask for an explanation.

For instance, if a member of your team uses the word *trust* several times in the course of a conversation, and you discern this to be of significant importance, you'd be wise to ask, "How do you know when someone is trustworthy?" This will give the individual the chance to clarify what trust means to him or her and to have it on the record. There's a great old saying from the world of communication training: "Words don't mean, people mean." You'd better believe it!

Determining meaning, then, is always an ongoing negotiation, not a commodity whose quality is guaranteed by the definitions in a dictionary. It requires both reflection and consideration. Reflection was not a part of our earlier sign-based, real-time processing of the world. The survival tasks we were engaged in then were much more concrete, and it was necessary for our signs to have a single meaning. As life grew increasingly complex, our verbal symbols gave language the portability it needed, along with a rich level of nuance that conveyed more subtle meanings.

In addition to cognitive meaning, communication also carries a component of emotional meaning, which we generally call the "feeling." We could define it as the color, tone, texture, and intensity of the sender's *emotional energy*. (Notice that all these descriptions are based in our sensations.) The urgency of our communicating is all about the feeling, the pressure of this energy. Here is where the nonverbal dimension becomes so incredibly important. We can say the words, "Wow, that's a nice dress!" to a coworker with any number of inflections. One way might elicit an appreciative "thank you!" even from the shiest person on the team. Another inflection might elicit a charge of sexual harassment. The way you use the tonality of your voice, the way you gesture and change your posture, the kind of face you make before and after you speak those words—all transmit emotional energy that adds feeling to the communication and helps determine the effect you have on the receiver and thus the response you get.

For your team's communication to be effective, you must integrate the meaning and the feeling components of your message. This requires synchronizing the verbal and nonverbal behavior, each of which is managed by a different brain structure. The limbic system is sometimes called the relational brain because it monitors the relationship between our internal and external worlds. It screens every face immediately for acceptance or rejection while simultaneously directing the immune system's ongoing crusade to determine which of the microbial life forms inside us are good and get to stay or harmful and have to go. The limbic structure includes the amygdala and hippocampus, brain centers that are responsible for forming, storing, and processing our memories of emotional events. The amygdala plays a highly significant role in coding fearful experiences so they will be uniquely memorable and in triggering the fight-or-flight response.

Wrapped around the limbic structure is the neocortex, which functions like a huge bank of random-access memory. That's the part of the brain responsible for performing executive functions such as comparing and contrasting complex options in decision making or imagining a completely novel way to solve a difficult problem. It is in this part of our brain (predominantly in the left hemisphere) that the construction and processing of language occurs.

When it all coordinates, your messages are descriptively complete and specific, as well as appropriately encoded with the emotional energy that tells your receiver how important the content is to you and how much and what type of importance you expect it to be given. Once your team members know what your proposed solution is and how strongly you feel, they know much better how to help accomplish it. This translates to a more productive team and a stronger bottom line.

Role

The fourth aspect of communication we address is the role of the communicators in the process. For teams working on increasing their ESI in communication, there are two roles they need to address. The senders initiate the communication, which gives them certain responsibilities, but the burden of successful communication is not theirs alone; receivers have important responsibilities as well. Communication does not occur all by itself. Both sender and receiver have certain responsibilities that must be respected for communication to take place.

The Sender's Responsibilities

Your desire to communicate with teammates is already a kind of request. You're asking them to give you their time and attention and to be receptive to your input. Ideally, it will be to their benefit to do so, but they really can't tell right off the bat. Obviously, having established a trusting relationship by having given them valuable information in the past will go a long way toward enhancing their receptivity. So it is important to proceed with the utmost respect of your team's resources. It's easier for people to lower their defenses with you when your communication behavior looks and sounds like theirs. Your familiarity with their reality makes you seem trustworthy, and this helps create a sense of psychological safety. The safer team members feel, the more effective and innovative their performance will be. Trying new ways to solve problems requires taking risks. When people feel safe and supportive on their team, they are much more likely to do this.

The sender builds safety by matching the volume, posture, pitch, and rate of speech with those of the receiver. This builds rapport, which is a kind of harmony or resonance. It's the feeling of "getting on the same page" or "being on the same wavelength."

One way to achieve this is to consider your receivers' biases and value filters and then prepare your message appropriately. Demonstrating the full measure of respect for your communication partner also requires that you make certain your message is as complete and specific as possible. There is a general rule of thumb you can use to help assess the completeness of your message. It must answer all parts of the question, "Who will do what for whom by when, and how specifically will it be done?" For example, "Avis, I want you to crunch those numbers in the new sales forecast and deliver them to marketing by noon on Friday. Display them in a report with two columns, the first showing last month's numbers and the second showing where we stand today." Communicating with this level of completeness and detail on important matters will significantly reduce misunderstanding in any relationship. When you start testing the quality of your messages by this standard, you'll begin to include the critical distinctions that will make your communication exponentially more effective.

However, don't lose sight of the fact that it is impossible for the tool of language ever to capture all of the detail present in your experience. To prove this, just start describing out loud everything you're aware of right now. See how much you can cover in one minute. Our direct experience of reality is simply too complex and too personal to be communicated. To talk about our experience, we must delete a significant amount of material and generalize or summarize much of the rest. Still, if you test your messages and those of your teammates with challenges such as "What specifically will we do?" and "How specifically will it be done?" it will make all your messages much easier for the receiver to receive and process regardless of their filters.

THE RECEIVER'S RESPONSIBILITIES

If it's at all possible that someone has some information that could help you achieve your personal or team goals more effectively, it will probably be worthwhile to give that person your full attention. It's also highly likely that most people who wish to communicate with you have not taken the time to figure out your filters and intentionally designed their communication for completeness. Even though these elements may be missing, you owe your teammate your respect. That respect is demonstrated by giving your full attention. Taking the time to focus on the message is also an excellent way to make your own time more productive.

Listening carefully can help you determine how much of your attention the issue really merits. This is especially true if you're communicating with someone with whom you have little or no relationship. Pay close attention, and you can rapidly discern whether or not this is something you want to spend time on or not. Also, if this is a member of your team or another person with whom you do have an ongoing relationship, it's very important to understand the message accurately—even if the sender botches the delivery. Sometimes one person may end up doing most of the work for both sides of the communication, but it never goes to waste. You and your team still benefit when the message is understood correctly, and the value the other person receives from your skillful example will help that person, whether aware of it or not.

The receiver's job is all about listening. Obviously, the receiver has to come up for air and speak sometimes, but an excellent receiver listens and listens and waits and waits, staying open to all the information that's forthcoming. If you do that, by the time you speak, you will have heard so much that you'll really have something important to say, something everybody else has probably missed. You will also command more attention from your teammates if you listen carefully and refrain from jumping in with a knee-jerk response. Be forewarned that it's not easy; here is the glitch.

What most people spend most of their time listening to is the voice inside their head. It's the voice of the announcer who is doing commentary about the sender or the voice that is already formulating a response and just waiting to pounce; whatever it is, it's not listening. Deepak Chopra (1991) said: "It's estimated that the average human has 60,000 thoughts a day. This is not surprising. What is disconcerting is that 90 percent of the thoughts you have today are the ones you had yesterday." That's not listening. Listening is almost a spiritual practice; it is similar to meditation in the focus and discipline it requires. It demands that you focus exclusively on someone else's reality.

You have to listen not just to the words that others are saying but also to the rate of their breathing while saying them. You have to listen to their elbows with your elbows, be in tune with their spine in your spine, look through their eyes with your eyes. If you listen even half this hard and give even half as good a reflection of the feelings and meanings that you hear, you will transform your team's experience of itself—guaranteed!

Knowledge is power, and listening is the fastest way to gain empowering information from your environment. Cross-reference the data you gain from actively listening with what you already know, and you'll synthesize new knowledge.

But your responsibility as a receiver doesn't end there. After listening, the pendulum swings the other way, and you become the sender. Now seek to send back the most accurate distillation of what you think you heard the sender say, giving the feedback in his or her own words, and see if you received it correctly.

Here's an example: "I know that the guys on the other marketing team are way behind on their campaign. They're still struggling to recover from the time they wasted designing a program for soccer moms, but they don't have a clue that I know, let alone who tipped me off."

That's what you, the receiver, think you heard, but you want to make sure you got it right, so you respond with something like this: "So *you* think they're way behind on their campaign and don't realize that anybody knows?" More than likely, what you'll hear back is something like "I *know* they are!"—because that's what was said in the first place. You received the message, boiled it down to the highlights, and gave feedback that distorted it just slightly (by saying "So *you think* . . ."), and that allows the sender to correct you while simultaneously underlining the essence of the message.

WHY DOES ALL THIS MATTER?

Communication matters when you're a member of a team and you and the team need to be more productive. It matters when you could get a raise if people knew how much you really do. It matters when you can't tell if you're accurately perceiving what's going on with your team or if you really need a reality check. It matters when you know there's something wrong but you can't figure out what it is and it could sabotage your team. It matters when you feel worried about the way things are going and could use some reassurance. It matters when you're bored or burnt out or feeling stale or have lost your edge or run dry. It matters whenever the stress and confusion and general craziness of this world get to be more than you can or want to tolerate—because communication is the first step in solving the next challenge that you feel is keeping you from having everything you need to be all that you can be. Whenever you have a moment in which you're brave enough to think about the challenges you face in your own future and those that will await your great-grandchildren, you will clearly understand why communication matters.

TIPS FOR GROWING YOUR TEAM'S COMMUNICATION SKILLS

- Active listening is a skill you can expand continuously. Many of you may have had some listening training. If your entire team hasn't had that training, consider it. More important, ask yourself how often the whole team uses active listening strategies. When a team member speaks about something valuable, listen with your head and your heart. Pay attention to the full communication—verbal and nonverbal—and then feed it back to double-check and validate your understanding. This is a particularly valuable endeavor when receiving a message from a team member with whom you don't get along so well. Building understanding will help nurture the relationship into more useful engagement.
- Let others know you have listened well by connecting what you understood to be their meaning and their feeling. Respond with a sentence along the lines of "You feel _____

because _____ ." The important part of this language pattern is to match the sender's emotion with the meaning of the content: "You feel upset because our manager comes to every meeting late" or "You are frustrated that the employee data aren't here because it means we can't finish our part of the project on time." If spoken with respect, your receiver will listen with interest and correct you if necessary. Just having the chance to hear the message back from someone else may help your teammate recognize a useful nuance to consider.

- At least once each meeting, practice acting from the opposite of your usual introverted or extroverted style. If you are an introvert, speak up one time more than you might naturally. If you are an extrovert, be quiet one extra time and give someone else, probably an introvert, a chance to speak.

- Consider using a more formal tool to evaluate how aware team members are of each other's feelings and how well they communicate the feeling and the meaning of their messages with each other. This is such an important process that we've developed a powerful tool to serve our clients, called the Collaborative Growth Team ESI (TESI) Survey. This and similar tools will help in determining how optimistic and how strong the team's identity is, whether team members feel motivated enough to succeed, and how honestly they will be able to resolve conflict. These benefits lead to one of the four critical results of employing ESI: trust. Trust is a result of reliably respectful and consistent behavior. As your team learns to take all of these steps more effectively, trust will grow, and it will become easier and more fun to perform well together.

CHAPTER SEVEN

THE FIFTH SKILL: STRESS TOLERANCE

Stress is an ignorant state. It believes that everything is an emergency.
NATALIE GOLDBERG

Bad weather had already put the foundation contractor behind schedule when the pour of a twelve-foot-high, hundred-foot-long wall ran into serious problems. Someone had missed some of the wedge bolts on a bottom panel of the wall. Nobody caught the oversight. The pour began. As the concrete filled the form, it swelled open and started to leak. By the time the carpenters noticed it, tons of concrete were bearing down on the leaking panel and threatened to blow it out.

One of them shouted to the boss to get a sheet of plywood and some two-by-eights as he ran toward an idling front-loader. When the other two carpenters saw their teammates running *away* from the pour, they signaled the cement mixer operator to stop. One ran toward the breach while the other grabbed the longest boards he could find. By the time he reached the sagging form with the boards, his teammate was kneeling on top of the twelve-foot-high wall reaching down for the first board. He stood up and thrust it between the forms, shoving and wiggling it as far down into the wet concrete as he could. Then he began pounding it as hard as he could. It was still three feet short of the bottom—it meant that he had accomplished nothing.

Suddenly, the cement truck driver appeared beside him on top of the form wall holding the vibrator up against the board, sinking it to the bottom and relieving the tremendous pressure.

Meanwhile, the boss had raced over with the four-by-eight sheet of three-quarter-inch plywood. The men placed it in position over the breach, and the other carpenters lined up the front-loader perpendicular to the wall where they could force the "patch" up against the leaking form and prevent the blowout. All this happened in less than ten minutes.

If that team hadn't responded so efficiently, the form would have exploded. Tons of concrete worth thousands of dollars would have solidified in a massive heap. They'd need jackhammers, loaders, and dump trucks to clean it up and haul it away to the recycling plant. Then they'd have to spend another two days to repair and ready the wall for another pour. Ten minutes' worth of high-performance teamwork under major stress saved the contractor several days and over $10,000.

WHAT STRESS TOLERANCE IS FOR TEAMS

Hans Seyle, one of the first researchers to address the topic of stress (1974), defined it as "the nonspecific response of the body to any demand for change." That is a great definition, but in these frenetic times, when one change follows hard and fast on another, stress can also be a euphemism for pain.

Stress tolerance is the skill of holding the world's parade of unpleasant surprises at bay. We can accomplish this best by using the early-warning system that our emotional awareness gives us, reading the emotional signals of our situation accurately, and responding to them effectively. There is also a strong physiological component to managing stress. Under closer examination, sometimes people discover that what they are doing to cope is little more than discharging their stress impulsively through anger, distraction, or self-medication. A better alternative is to stand your body up on a treadmill and use the very same energy to jog a couple of miles. That not only releases the stress but also increases the body's ability to drive oxygen deeper and deeper into the cells, where it can metabolize the stress toxins that build up there.

Teams have to do more to develop stress tolerance. They have the added responsibility of needing to observe and learn how each of their fellow team members automatically responds to stress. It is this automatic response that proves so problematic for teams and individuals because it is deeply wired into our behavior. It automatically cranks into gear when we encounter stimuli in the world that are threatening—the sound of your mother-in-law's voice when she gets "that tone," the look that means the boss isn't happy, and similar signals that you receive when someone's needs have not been met or someone's expectations have been disappointed and you are responsible.

One of the most enduring ways to build stress tolerance is by building strong relationships among team members. That takes time, effort, flexibility, trust, and every so often a dose of forgiveness. As you learn how to respond to each other in stress, you become more aware of your own behavior patterns. With that key information in hand, you can start rewiring those patterns.

THE SEVEN INGREDIENTS OF STRESS TOLERANCE FOR TEAMS

In our work we have found that the following seven ingredients combine nicely in a variety of recipes for reducing and managing stress, both in the workplace and in our personal lives. We urge you to engage this material with special attention because it pertains so directly to everyone's physical health.

1. *Environmental awareness.* Maintaining a clear awareness of both your physical and your social environments will provide you with a steady stream of essential information about what to move toward and want to move away from—and how rapidly you need to move! Stress is ultimately a physiological cost. It's your body that really pays the dues, even though you may personally experience a substantial amount of emotional angst from the various stresses of your life. To some extent, your ability to accurately read what is expected of you in the social environment actually determines how much stress you experience.

The other people in your life expect certain kinds of behavior from you based on your culture and their historical relationship with you. Because of the long period of investment humans make in their children while they are young and dependent, adults generally expect children to start learning the behaviors that contribute to family and community support as soon as their children are old enough to begin imitating them. The quality of early training each team member received will have a strong impact on your team.

Being conscious of and regulating the emotional pressures in your social environment and the physical tensions in your body gives you the ability to manage stress instead of being swamped by it. You can do this as you become more and more adept at listening to your internal and external world. Attentive listening enables you to determine what you and the people around you are feeling and why. When you listen to yourself and reflect on your own sensory and emotional experience, that skill is called emotional self-awareness. When you respond with compassion or understanding to a teammate's stress, you are using the emotional intelligence called empathy. To read feelings accurately, you need to silence the cognitive chatter in your mind and resensitize your awareness to the subtle messages you are constantly receiving from your body and the field of social relationships around you. Focusing your attention on your breath is one of the easiest techniques for doing this. The purpose is not to get the insight you need to figure out how to drive things better, it's to allow yourself to back off so that you can be steered!

2. *Assertiveness.* When you have accurately sensed what is going on and why, the next step in stress management is to tell the team what you learned. For instance, if your boss gave a promised project to a colleague, you might say, "I feel disrespected because you promised that work to me and then gave it to someone else." This kind of self-disclosure amounts to "taking your emotional pulse in public," and the more comfortable team members feel in doing this, the better your team will function. Stating your own emotional reality provides immediate feedback to your team that team members can synthesize and respond to right away. It's efficient.

It's accurate. It takes the guesswork out of the equation. You don't have to hope that your team will figure it out, and your teammates don't have to hope that they can read your mind. It's your responsibility to tell people what you need and want.

Of course, self-disclosure can be a risky business. No wonder it's so important to spend time building relationships and deepening trust. The other critical factor is functional, adult communication. The stronger your team's communication skills, the easier it is to be assertive. Coaches and consultants can do wonders in facilitating a shorter learning curve for these skills. Their expertise and objectivity can move your team to a higher level of performance faster than any other strategy.

3. *Self-regard.* Self-regard calls for us to accept ourselves, warts and all. The only way people can change their behaviors and work more successfully together as a team is if they feel confident that they are valued by the team. They have to feel a substantial level of psychological safety within the team and be able to trust that even if they make a mistake, they won't be punished. This is a specific example of how teams can (and must) help their members meet the second-level safety needs that Maslow mentioned.

Unfortunately, many of us learned that making mistakes can be costly to our self-image and esteem—that we will be embarrassed if someone notices our shortcomings. Hence we are reluctant to be exposed in front of the people whose support we need most; this builds risk intolerance, which reduces a team's closeness, creativity, and ultimate productivity. People generally don't like to admit to much imperfection, but feeling obliged to keep up an unrealistic facade is often precisely what pumps up the stress.

When a team member makes a mistake, accountability is appropriate. A mistake is an opportunity to teach and learn. Both are valuable. If mistakes are punished with embarrassment and social rejection, rather than corrected through teaching and learning strategies, then self-regard, creativity, and innovative risk taking all plummet.

On high-functioning teams, all members respect and care for the self-regard of each team member. That's what gives the team a sense of identity and makes the members feel that they want to belong to the team. You know your colleagues will step in for you when the chips are down. You know they are looking out for you, and although they may offer constructive feedback about your performance within the team, you know that they would never criticize you publicly.

4. *Wellness.* Because stress endangers your physical health, high-performance teams value wellness and check in regularly with strategies for supporting their team members' physical and mental health. This has to be done elegantly so that it does not come across as judgmental. To take an easy example, a team member who is obviously overweight is likely to be uncomfortable with questions about what everyone had for dinner last night! And yet if the team is genuinely respectful and supportive of all members in their attempts to improve their health, individuals may feel safe and even inspired to undertake significant changes in their daily routines. These acts of health building may start a virtuous circle that inspires other team members to pursue new fitness goals of their own. One example of how to be a supportive teammate is to bring carrot sticks or cucumber slices to a meeting instead of junk food, especially if you know someone is dieting.

5. *Humor.* When the going gets tough, the tough can laugh at themselves. Laughter actually stimulates the production of "feel-good" endorphins, strengthens the immune function, and reduces the levels of highly corrosive stress hormones such as cortisol and epinephrine. Norman Cousins (1964) demonstrated how powerful this can be when he discovered that he could manage the pain of a severe degenerative disease of the spine by watching movies that gave him a deep belly laugh.

In addition to the neurochemical benefits of laughter, humor helps us refocus our perspective. Jokes are funny because they surprise our expectations. Humor not only helps teams manage stress but also helps them create innovative approaches for solving problems. Teams function more effectively when their members heed the popular adage "He who laughs . . . lasts!"

6. *Flexibility.* To be able to bend without breaking in the daily winds of change at work is a critical ingredient of stress tolerance for teams. The exercises we see people doing at the gym are designed to develop one of three qualities: strength, which is achieved through pumping iron; endurance, which is accomplished on the treadmill or stationary bike; and flexibility, which is accomplished on the floor mats through yoga and other forms of stretching.

The value of strength in a team is reflected in the parable that it is impossible to break a bundle of ten sticks all at once but quite easy to break them one at a time. When a team is known to speak with a single voice, it gains credibility and influence. For instance, if the workload that a team is expected to accomplish is unreasonable, it is far more persuasive for everyone to challenge it together in a meeting than just to send the "group leader" in to discuss it with the boss.

By knowing each other's strengths, complementing them, and working together, the team achieves its power. However, this kind of strength is not as valuable as endurance and flexibility from the perspective of stress tolerance. Endurance in the workplace today can actually best be enhanced by more periods of rest. So many people at work have been running so hard for so long that they are literally exhausted. Chronic exhaustion diminishes the power of the team because it saps members of resilience, creativity, and stress tolerance.

Physical flexibility comes from stretching a set of muscles just a little bit farther each day. It makes the muscles stronger, but even more important, it gives you the ability to bend and reach to the full extent of your capacity. This is what it takes to be able to adapt to change. This is what it takes to be able to envision new strategies and novel solutions to the problems in the workplace. This is what it takes to be able to adjust to a global marketplace fueled by an ongoing explosion of knowledge and unparalleled technological advantages. Our species has had no chance to adapt physically or emotionally to the world our intellectual prowess has created. Consequently, the incredible pace of innovation and transference of knowledge are also increasingly compromising the life support systems of our planet and eroding the depth and quality of family relationships. We're all too tired, and we're all too wired. In such an environment, it is essential to be able to bend and not break. Your team will provide a great gift to your organization if it can model this kind of flexibility and resilience.

7. *Humility.* This is probably one of the most powerful ingredients of stress tolerance, but it is also one of the most advanced. Jim Collins pointed out in *Good to Great* (2001) that humility shows up in great leaders as the ability to attribute successes to the people around them while personally taking responsibility for the failures. The ability to add this ingredient to the recipe for stress tolerance means that a team member has worked diligently to develop a larger, more comprehensive vision of life. That person has learned how to weave together the experiences, relationships, and priorities in life to produce whatever is most meaningful and valuable. A humble person realizes that it's impossible to do this without the help of others and that sometimes circumstances will thwart even the best of efforts. Yet overall perseverance will produce the best results possible, and that will be enough.

WHY TEAMS NEED STRESS TOLERANCE

The alarm clock is ringing. Larry groans, fumbles, knocks his watch off the nightstand, and finally manages to silence it. Suddenly, he jerks awake and scrambles out of bed. He just remembered he is presenting his summary of the research-and-development report to the entire department today. He starts the coffee and jumps in the shower.

"Man, I've got to nail it today—this is absolutely critical!" he says to himself. "The bigwigs are going to be there for this one!

I've just got to change their minds. Yeah, right, as if those morons had any minds at all."

He dresses rapidly, too nervous to tie his tie properly until the fourth try. It's new, and so is the suit; he pays a lot of money for his clothes. He's into the "dress for success" strategy. When he gives himself a final glance in the mirror, it really does look like his hair is thinning. "Oh, great, I'm already falling apart!" he thinks, shaking his head as he dashes to the kitchen and pours the Colombian dark roast into his stainless steel travel mug.

He grabs his briefcase and jumps into the car. Half a block down the road, he realizes that the handouts he prepared are still stacked on his desk, not in the briefcase. At the stop sign, he honks repeatedly at the car in front of him, does a U-turn, and races back home. He grabs the stack of papers and shuffles through them nervously to see if they're all there.

As you can imagine, the rest of the drive to work goes about the same way. By the time Larry reaches his office, he's sweating lightly but continuously, and he's edgy with everyone. His pulse is racing, his stomach is burning and churning. His breathing is shallow, and a couple of times he thinks he's actually feeling some pain in his chest, but that's crazy—he's only thirty-six.

Luis pops his head around the corner of his cubicle and says the meeting's been moved up half an hour. Larry freaks. "Who the hell's idea is that?"

"I know this is totally upsetting, man; it seems completely unfair," Luis replies reassuringly. "I'll see if I can find out why it got moved and if there's any way we can get together at the scheduled time. Meanwhile, if you review the slideshow you've done, I think that'll help you chill out some. You've got some powerful information in there, and I think reviewing it will help reassure you."

Larry reaches for his coffee cup, but Luis takes hold of it first. "You don't need any more java, man. I'll bring you back some water, or would you rather have juice?"

"Um, water is fine. You're right; I'm already wired," Larry nods.

Luis goes straight to his cubicle and calls Morgan, the team lead, on her cell phone. "Code red—Larry's in meltdown," he says. "You should probably stop by his cube. Do you know why the meeting's been moved up half an hour? When I told him that, I think it was the last straw."

"I'm not sure," Morgan replies. "I think it's coming down from upstairs. After I talk to Larry, I'll see if there's anything we can do, but in the meantime, I want you to go to the conference room and make absolutely certain that the projector is set up and ready to function perfectly. You know how flustered he gets if there are any foul-ups. Also, if you see Jared, have him stop by to see Larry; he does pretty well with Larry at times like this."

Jared is already in the conference room working when Luis gets there. He tells Jared about their teammate's freakout, and Jared says he'll go check in. Larry is avidly reviewing his slideshow when Jared arrives.

"Hey, what's going on? You're the man!" Jared reaches out and gives Larry a solid handshake.

"Some idiot has rescheduled the meeting half an hour earlier!" Larry shoots back.

"Someone probably just can't wait to hear the good news you've got," he replies.

"Good news? Why do you say that?" Larry asks. "Who thinks it's good news?"

"Everybody, or nearly everybody," Jared answers. "No one in the organization likes all the hassles in the current process, and the word on the street is that you've got a better way."

"You're kidding. Who thinks that?" Larry asks skeptically.

"Well, obviously, all of us on the team are convinced, and we think you'll be able to convince the big boss. Your presentation is pretty compelling—but right now you look totally stressed out. I thought you'd be psyched about this. What's going on?" Jared sounds truly concerned.

"Some lady was practically asleep at a stop sign today while she was talking on her cell phone, and I nearly hit her. Then she just dawdled off like nothing happened."

"Yeah, the way other people drive can be a major headache," Jared agrees. "But you're way too wound up now to do a good job with *our* presentation."

"What the hell do you mean?" Larry snaps back.

"That's just exactly what I mean!" Jared replies. "Whatever upset you has still got your goat, and that was hours ago. You've got to decompress to do your best this morning. The whole team is counting on you to make us look good. Since you're feeling so feisty, let's arm-wrestle and use up some of that extra energy."

"That's totally stupid!" Larry replies.

"So you're a chicken, too," Jared quips. "I'll bet that disoriented old lady at the stop sign would have kicked your butt if you'd been brave enough to get out of your car! Come on, let's arm-wrestle."

And so they do. And although Larry is no match for the former linebacker, the release he gets feels so good that he agrees to climb the stairs with Jared for ten or fifteen minutes to burn off some more of his stress. By the time he gets back to his cubicle, Morgan is coming around looking for him for the second time.

"Hi, Larry," she says. "I wasn't able to get the time of the meeting changed back. It's something from upstairs, but I'd be happy to sit down with you for twenty minutes or so and review your slideshow. I see you've got it up."

"Really?" Larry asks, much calmer now. "That would be great."

So they spend the remaining time going over the presentation, and whenever Larry starts to get nervous, Morgan reminds him to take a breath. By the second run-through, he has it down. His nervousness is gone.

Larry goes on to give a stellar presentation to the executive team. The praise from the CEO is particularly rewarding. He says he's impressed by the creative ideas and the concise solution for eliminating the bottleneck that has consistently thwarted production goals.

HOW THE TEAM APPLIED THE SEVEN INGREDIENTS

Larry almost self-destructed, which would have destroyed the credibility of the team and tainted the merits of the project. However, his emotionally intelligent teammates helped get him back in balance, and thanks to those efforts, the entire team benefited.

Using his environmental awareness, Luis realized instantly that Larry was freaking out. They had all seen it before. So Luis's response was both compassionate and outcome-oriented.

He and the rest of the team needed Larry to give a compelling presentation, and Larry's ability to do that would not be furthered by his drinking more coffee. Luis used a tactful and respectful approach to get Larry to start nourishing himself instead of fueling his agitation with caffeine.

Luis also did an excellent job of using his empathy to establish rapport by matching Larry's general tonality while reflecting that he understood Larry's meaning and why he was so tense.

By saying, "I know this is totally upsetting, man; it seems completely unfair," Luis let Larry know he understood Larry's distress, but he didn't melt down along with Larry. He also redirected Larry's attention to the resources represented by the slideshow, which could help Larry reconnect with his feelings of self-regard.

Morgan, the team leader, was also practical and resourceful. Although she couldn't really do much about Larry's state at the moment, she knew she could help prevent it from deteriorating further by having Luis ensure that the technical equipment was running properly. When she got to the office, she too redirected Larry's attention to what was going right (the positive process he outlined in the slideshow). This not only refreshed his feelings of self-regard but also got him focused on the material he would have to present shortly.

Of all his fellow team members, Jared single-handedly (literally!) gave him the most useful gift. Jared could tell that as stressed as Larry was, he needed some kind of physical activity to focus his attention and burn off some of the stressful energy that was building up inside. Jared's use of humor in that playful challenge to arm-wrestle was perfect. This gave Larry a way to convert the stress into physical activity, and when that felt good, Larry agreed to climb some stairs, which was even better because it increased his oxygen level.

ADDITIONAL BENEFITS

Stress-tolerant teams are able to avoid the self-destruction that can occur when internal mistakes and workplace pressures trigger other teams to criticize and attack each other.

The flexibility that is part of stress tolerance gives the team bench strength. When members know each other well, they can work with each other in different capacities. This is a great perk because it fosters cross-functionality. Team members can fill in at critical times. An unexpected absence is no longer a crisis.

THE DOWNSIDES

Although listening is a basic element for cultivating environmental awareness, it can be an excuse for inactivity. A team can allow itself to become mired in indecision when listening is used as a tactic to avoid dealing with conflict. Virtually every decision that teams must make is done without having all the information the group would like. The information may not exist, may be too costly to obtain, or may take too long to get. There is a point beyond which waiting for more data or waiting because something is difficult or perceived to be too delicate results in nothing but missed opportunities.

Too much flexibility can mean that your team (or one of its members) ends up doing someone else's work instead of fulfilling its assigned responsibilities. You or a teammate might be too likely to say, "Sure, I can do that." You say that because in theory you *could* do it. Your flexibility jumps in before your time management and reality-testing skills have a chance to protest! So much of the pressure in the workplace has to do with meeting challenging or even irrational deadlines that managing time well turns out to be one of a team's most powerful stress tolerance practices.

Excessive or unrealistic self-regard gives rise to the short-sightedness of self-importance. Egocentric thinking that does not consider the needs and motives of everyone involved fails to anticipate risks and opportunities that can significantly affect a team. If insecurity drives your need for recognition, you are likely to overlook an opportunity where someone else could take the credit and gain favor with an ally who can champion the team.

Too much assertiveness is a euphemism for bullying; trust erodes, team members feel disrespected, and people look for jobs elsewhere.

The mixture of high levels of optimism and stress tolerance can be such a rich fuel that without appropriate reality testing, team members lose perspective on the other aspects of their lives. Because there is so much to do and they feel like they are getting so much done, family values and work-life balance get out of kilter, resulting in an obsessive concentration on business. You may then experience a big case of burnout. This is literally an example of too much of a good thing.

TIPS FOR GROWING YOUR TEAM'S STRESS TOLERANCE

- In the core of your being, accept and endorse the fact that a group of people will always be smarter than any one of you.
- Realize that the group can be an unparalleled support and resource for all of you once you all build the appropriate levels of trust, mutual respect, and accountability.
- Invite the appropriate confrontation and challenge for your own ideas. Ask questions like "What do you think I might have overlooked?" "How will the competition respond?" and "Is there anything that will keep this from working in the long term?" This stimulates the team members' problem-solving skills, builds assertiveness, and generates direct rather than roundabout discussions. Inviting criticism is an excellent way of modeling how confident team members behave.
- Practice the "You feel _____ because _____ " model for respectfully expressing empathy. The more closely you listen and observe, the more accurately you will be able to reflect to your team members what they feel and why, and the better you will be able to understand what makes your team hum. You'll gain an intimate understanding of what motivates, inspires, and frustrates your teammates.
- All of these efforts are designed for one purpose—to help your fellow team members build their self-regard through your pointing out to them what they do well and can feel good about. As authentic self-regard grows among your teammates, their defensiveness retreats, and they become more open, more effective communicators. This kind of self-confidence is crucial for increasing stress tolerance.

- Reduce stress by expanding your team's options. Develop problem-solving flexibility by making it part of your team culture to invite or even require multiple solutions for major issues. For instance, ask, "If we couldn't do it that way, what could we do?" This may seem a little silly initially, but the first time your team comes up with a better idea on the second round, everyone will be much more curious and excited to conduct this exercise. And if you can be playful while you consider options, the stress level can be kept in check.
- Develop team rituals like a motto, a handshake and a cheer, a logo, a team hat or flag. It's a way of creating your team brand. This might seem preposterous given the amount of work you have to do, but the energy you will sustain from strengthening this kind of behavior will more than make up for the time spent on it. Invent a guardian spirit for your team that keeps the time wasters away (or whatever sorts of demons plague your team). Then develop a chant or rhyme to invoke it and to do so with great solemnity at the start of every team meeting.
- If you aren't comfortable with rituals, you might instead develop a sort of pledge of allegiance in which you proclaim your commitment to the team values—honesty, accountability, playfulness, whatever. The attitude of ceremonial dignity with which you endow it will bond all the team members at a much deeper level. Bringing out the kid in each of you helps your team be more playful and creative and, consequently, less stressed. Everyone's subconscious mind is seven years old and loves this kind of stuff! And if you think your elite self-reflective conscious mind is what is running the show, just try to secrete the right amount of pancreatin on command next time you eat or try to dilate your eyes on purpose when you leave a dark room and move into the sunlight. It's impossible!

Once you get all your seven-year-olds playing happily together, no matter how long or challenging the task, you'll have lots more energy and fun. It is estimated that adults laugh only about fifteen times a day, whereas children laugh four hundred times. Let's wise up and take the cure! Our prescription is more play and laughter—it's a proven winner for health, creativity, and stress tolerance!

Chapter Eight

The Sixth Skill: Conflict Resolution

Sit down and be quiet.
You are drunk, and this is the edge of the roof.
Rumi

The western United States conjures up images of the gold rush, cowboys on horseback, and stagecoaches being held up by gun-slinging outlaws. That's Hollywood. The real West is all about water. The battles are about how it's used, where it goes, and who gets it. The law is very clear: the first one to use the water gets it. It sounds simple, but that law was created when the population was a fraction of what it is now. Today, California has a larger claim on the water in the Colorado River than Colorado itself, even though Colorado contributes about 70 percent of the water in the river and California doesn't contribute any. Some ranchers have all the water they need, every year, regardless of other needs, while downstream neighbors lose crops to drought.

The controversies are fierce. Marcia knows firsthand. She was general counsel to the Metropolitan Water Providers for more than a dozen years. The Providers were a consortium of more than forty Denver metropolitan cities and water and sanitation districts seeking to increase the metro Denver water supply. They proposed building Two Forks Dam and Reservoir and invested over $40 million and thirteen years in the effort. The proposal became the flashpoint for water rights and related concerns. Environmentalists objected to changing the ecosystem and to growth of the metropolitan area. Some recreation advocates didn't want the water's flow to be diverted; others could hardly wait for a new lake with boating and fishing to be developed in the semiarid state. Regulatory entities from local, state, and federal agencies were called on for permitting decisions. It was as contentious a time as any in Colorado's colorful history.

As the firestorm heated up, Colorado's governor, Richard Lamm, led an extraordinary team effort by creating the Governor's Metropolitan Water Supply Roundtable. He brought in the water providers, environmentalists, and representatives from other parts of the state whose water supply would be changed due to the proposed diversion of the water. He also brought in the metropolitan area's home builders, neighborhood groups, and financial leaders.

It was an august body, working on the most visible, contentious, and profoundly important issue in the western United States. The stakes were extremely high. Governor Lamm recognized this and demanded the highest decorum from participants. They had to agree to hear each other out. They had to consent to engaging in civil discourse and exploring alternatives. They did. Difficult points were navigated, and new understandings were forged.

The roundtable was a mechanism for building relationships and understandings. However, it ran into difficulties. The rules of decorum, while making for polite conversation, also stifled the group. The discussions were safe. They became paralyzed by overanalysis. When the group finally tried to move toward creating a specific proposal, communication faltered, and the fragile truce broke down. At the same time that the roundtable got stuck, the governor completed his third and final term. Roy Romer, the next governor, assumed the role of permit decision maker instead of cultural communication broker. Without the governor's leadership, the fragile cooperation between adversarial teams broke down.

WHAT CONFLICT RESOLUTION IS FOR TEAMS

We define team conflict as a challenge involving disagreement based on different perspectives, values, and priorities that gains enough energy to perturb the system. Conflict resolution is the process employed by the individuals and teams facing the challenge to resolve the matter. Many styles of resolution can be used, including cooperation, confrontation, competition, and the most sophisticated, collaboration.

Conflict comes from the Latin root *confligere*, which means "to strike together." The work of conflict resolution is to help people move from striking together to working cooperatively, or akin to what Fisher and Ury (1981) would say, moving from no to yes. Conflict is as evident in nature as it is in society. The delicate balance of the food chain is maintained by conflict. The earth's ecosystems are renewed by conflict. Water and wind carve new canyons; fire destroys forests to allow for their regeneration; evaporation of water reseeds the clouds, bringing water to thirsty crops.

Conflict is always an opportunity. We are engaged in an increasingly complex world, which often increases conflict or makes resolution more complicated. For teams to function well in this dynamic environment, they need to be operating with clearly articulated values and ethics governing their decisions and actions. Your response to the challenges and opportunities brought by conflict can have a truly evolutionary impact on a broad scale—for yourself, for your teams, for organizations, and even the whole world.

Futurist Jennifer James (1996, pp. 67–68) writes, "The biggest mistake we can make in trying to predict patterns and trends is to have too narrow a focus. . . . Chaos theory is the science of process, the knowledge of what is becoming, not what is or will remain. Our minds and our businesses are not always systems in balance; they are always in process. Just try to trace a thought back to its genesis. Do the same with your business product or service."

When you're willing to entertain change and conflict, giving up much of the illusion that you're in control, you and your team can actually find powerful new levels of success. It's a modern-day form of risk taking based on recognizing interconnectedness and expanding your awareness.

Peter Russell, a theoretical physicist and author of *Waking Up in Time* (1992), clarifies the breathtaking, confusing, and all but overwhelming rate of change with which we're living.

The ever-increasing pace of change we're now experiencing, he states, is due to the fact that today, "technological breakthroughs spread through society in years rather than centuries. Calculations that would have taken decades are now made in minutes. Communication that once required months occurs in seconds. Development in every area is happening faster and faster" (p. 3). The bottom line is that this incredibly rapid pace of change means that humans—and teams—have to be more adaptable and more agile. They have to be more flexible, more willing to address conflict readily and directly, and at its first signs, not after team members have dug in and taken intractable positions.

We suggest that teams embrace a "chaordic" way of being. Dee Hock, founder and former CEO of the VISA credit card company, coined this term to refer to a system that is simultaneously chaotic and ordered. The goal, of course, is to find a harmonious balance between these two characteristics, with neither chaos nor order dominating.

The team skill of conflict resolution measures how willing the team is to engage in conflict openly and constructively. If your team isn't strong in handling conflict, it suggests the teammates may be conflict-averse or tend to personalize conflict rather than separating personal preferences and behavior from the problem. One of the first commandments for resolving conflict effectively is to critique the work, not the person, and to identify specific suggestions for improvement. If your team members handle conflict pretty well, you can usually engage each other and tackle problems effectively as they arise. This also means that you and your teammates accept correction without holding grudges or taking revenge on people who have criticized you. If you are a member of a remarkable team that builds its skills in actively appreciating the value of conflict as a strategic way to develop strong resilient solutions, count yourself exceptionally fortunate.

THE NINE INGREDIENTS OF TEAM CONFLICT RESOLUTION

Conflict occurs in many guises for teams. It can be as minor as deciding the agenda order for a meeting or when to take a lunch break or as major as the need to confront a highly competent colleague who has behaved in an outrageous or offensive way. Here is a list of the nine most important tools in your team's repertoire for handling conflict. Keep in mind that it takes great effort to hone some of these skills. Don't expect to implement them all immediately. Expect that there will be times when your team is employing four or five of these tools and not all nine. Don't panic. Adding even one or two of the most important skills can boost the success of your efforts significantly. There is no endpoint in the conflict resolution skill development process. As people come and go, your team will keep evolving. Remember: the goal is not to achieve perfection but to have a positive learning attitude.

1. *Patience.* What a challenge it can be to listen to your teammate go on endlessly about his or her take on a situation. People want to be heard more than they want to be right. There is simply no shortcut to the requirement that you respect your teammates. High-performing teams listen to their members with open minds. If you *choose* to be impatient, you are *deciding* to pay the consequences. Patience is a skill that you can cultivate. Impatience is a choice. You don't get off the hook by saying, "I'm just not a patient person."

2. *Perspective.* Most people are well aware that perspectives vary. Most realize that one person's take on the best strategy for selling widgets will be different from someone else's strategy. Usually those differences go unnoticed. They're commonplace. However, add deep conflict into the mix, and it's a different dynamic. Team members need to appreciate the unique perspective each person brings to an issue in order to leverage conflict to the best outcome. Differing perspectives can be your team's greatest strength if you treat them as ideas or possibilities, or they can be your team's downfall if you butt heads over them.

3. *Intention and attention.* Want to solve conflict well? Start by being a member of a team where everyone has the personal *intention* to work together as a team and to find the best possible solutions with the resources at your disposal. Then make a list of what you need to pay *attention* to—your criteria, a checklist to keep you focused. Writing out a list of specific

items that you check on regularly is the best way to make sure your intention, like a New Year's resolution, doesn't evaporate in just a few weeks.

4. *Collaborative communication.* Patience, perspective, and intention and attention are essential but not sufficient. You also have to have a shared commitment to spend the time required to work through issues. An openness to collaboration shows that you value yourself, your work, and your team enough to be willing to engage in the conflict. Avoiding hard issues is tempting, but ignoring them can sound the death knell for a team.

5. *Empathy.* Showing care, concern, and respect are all powerful ways to boost a team's effectiveness. One way to work through a conflict on your team is by letting your teammates know that you are seriously considering what they are advocating, that you will attend to their perspectives, and that you respect their opinions and feelings. This kind of empathy can profoundly change the team dynamics. Simple acts of compassion facilitate the most difficult conversations and allow the team to find ways to move forward.

6. *Assertiveness.* One of the most difficult and most culturally contextualized ESI behaviors is assertiveness. You're assertive when you speak up and express your concerns, desires, and perspectives. Steven Stein and Howard Book in *The EQ Edge* (2000) discuss the balance needed to express assertiveness well. It's found in the happy medium between being passive, which is the failure to speak up regarding an important issue, and being aggressive, which is expressing your point of view in a manner that takes it too far, leaving your teammates no room to disagree. The volume and tone of your voice, along with your posture, gestures, facial features, and other non-verbal signals, play a big role in this, because empathy and assertiveness need to be blended for effective teamwork. Aim to engage conflict with what we call empathic assertiveness.

7. *Choice in conflict resolution style.* Does your team have a predictable style for resolving conflict? Your response might be anything from "You bet!" or "We don't" to "The boss just tells us" or "We talk and choose something in between, through give and take."

Individuals and teams have a range of choices for dealing with conflict. The strongest teams are flexible, able to choose the style that fits the situation. Kenneth Thomas and Ralph Kilmann created a simple yet effective tool known as the Thomas-Kilmann Instrument in the 1970s. The five key styles of responding to conflict they identified are avoiding, accommodating, compromising, competing, and collaborating.

Strong teams are adept at using all five ways. Not every conflict demands the same approach. Teams, like individuals, need choice in responses to conflicts. If a team took up every potential conflict, nothing of substance would get done. However, if you ignore critical issues, your team will underperform or fail. As the saying goes, it's all about knowing when to hold 'em and when to fold 'em. You have to be able to identify the important issues and be willing to deal with them while letting trivial matters go so you don't lose focus.

8. *Humor.* Used wisely, there's probably no better antidote to conflict than a good dose of humor. Of course, it backfires if people take the humorous comment as a put-down or as a clue that they don't have to take the matter seriously. Humor must be used with sensitivity and a good sense of timing. With that understood, lighten up! Ask each other just how serious the issue is. Will it matter in five days, five months, or five years? Gaining perspective is worth its weight in gold.

9. *Gratitude.* Recognizing and celebrating the many gifts you receive as a team is the foundation of your resilience. You also build rapport with one another when you take even a few seconds to express your gratefulness to others. Make gratitude a habit. Be deliberate about building this one up if it isn't already a team strength. Even if you're just grateful for one thing one of your team members does, you are improving the climate for collaboration when you express your thanks.

WHY TEAMS NEED CONFLICT RESOLUTION SKILLS

Not a single board member wanted to attend the board meetings of the Community Health Care Association (CHCA) anymore.

Some were worn out by the state of affairs; others were worried or angry. No one was happy or hopeful.

Javier, the newly installed executive director who'd been on the job for nine months, was losing sleep. He knew that a conflicted board could not solve problems well or provide the community leadership the organization needed. He called Roseanne, the CEO of the local nonprofit consortium, who agreed to meet for lunch the following day.

As they sat down, Javier got right to the point. "Roseanne, I've got a huge problem. There's a divisive split on the board about our fundraising strategy. Both camps have dug their heels in, and I don't know how to move either side."

Roseanne nodded knowingly. "This has got to be tough for you. Managing volunteer boards is one of the most delicate and most difficult jobs around. I hate it when they get stuck, don't you?"

Javier nodded and sighed. "I just don't know what to do. One camp wants to take what we've done in the past and continue to build relationships and get donations based on the groundwork we've laid. The other camp says it's a waste of time and wants to really shake things up. They're proposing we cancel the Sweetheart Ball and just do power breakfasts with groups such as the local home builders association and the *Fortune* 500 companies in the area and ask for donations. What in the heck can I do?"

"What strategies have you used so far?" Roseanne asked.

Javier proceeded to give her the details. He told her that at first he thought the board members were just testing one another, so he avoided making a big deal out of it. When it just got worse, he set a meeting with the board chair, Nanette, to brainstorm ideas. They decided that if they presented a concrete plan of action to the board, members would feel more focused and less like each one of them had to chart the course of the organization independently. They hoped to build a collaborative spirit around a central goal of fundraising at the annual ball.

"How'd that go?" Roseanne asked hopefully.

"Not well." Javier put his head in his hands. "That effort actually seemed to propel them into the two camps."

"This *is* tough," Roseanne agreed. "Let's walk back to my office; we can brainstorm along the way." She set a brisk pace to get Javier's energy flowing again. Sharing some of her experience, she helped Javier craft a plan around gaining the support of the executive team, as there were representatives from both camps on that committee. These members had long histories with the board, and Roseanne gave him tips on how to win their support.

When he got back to his office, Javier called Nanette and the executive committee, asking them to come together to tackle the issue directly and develop solutions to take back to the board. Javier began with hopeful gratitude: "Thanks for your involvement with CHCA and for helping us find an answer to this challenge." He was direct. "Without your help in getting the board all on the same page, the organization will fold. If we can't resolve this fundraising issue, our mission is in jeopardy."

He took them through the organization's financial position and showed them two sets of financial projections—one with a successful fundraising effort and one without. It was sobering. The committee pondered what he'd said and met again several days later. "Surely we share one overriding common goal: to promote the organization and help with successful fundraising," Nanette emphasized. "Let's not second-guess the board; let's first build agreement about the need to get on the same page and then consider alternatives."

It was an interesting discussion. Jacob and Stephen still wanted power breakfasts; they wanted to be new and modern. Jacob suddenly seemed to hear his cantankerous tone and softened a bit. "You know," he said, "we're killing this organization with our own separate styles of seeking success." Everyone looked at him in surprise. Jacob had been the most vehement in fighting for the new way. "Maybe I've been getting too big for my britches. This may not be the right kind of strategy for this kind of organization. The only reason I volunteered is because I want to see the mission work. Tell me," he asked, looking at the people who favored the traditional ball, "if we all get behind this event and make it the best darn ball we've ever had, would you then come back and work with us on some new strategies soon after that?" Board members were so relieved that they began eagerly agreeing and recognizing Jacob for a leadership skill they hadn't seen in him before.

The board meeting went remarkably well. All participants were able to rally around their shared purpose and gain a new perspective. At the end of the meeting, the board members laughed and expressed their gratitude. "Wow," they said to one another, "at last we've got a plan. Thanks!"

HOW THE TEAM APPLIED THE NINE INGREDIENTS

The team used the nine ingredients. Javier recognized the severity of the conflict and was assertive about resolving it. He demonstrated empathy and gratitude in working with the executive committee and was able to move the executives to a place where they could seek collaborative communication.

The committee members gained clarity about their intention and the need to work together well. Their work set an example for the entire board. This led the board to begin gaining perspective and find common ground. Jacob's surprise turnaround added a bit of humor and changed the style they'd used previously for coping with conflict.

Of course, the high level of ESI demonstrated by Roseanne really helped Javier. She gave the problem her full attention and empathy. She also generously shared her wisdom, garnered from years of experience, and mentored Javier.

All of this led to a renewed collaborative spirit within the board. By verbalizing recognition and appreciation of the breakthrough, the board members were sowing seeds of hope that could serve them in their next encounter with conflict. Their patience in staying with one another through the challenge was rewarded with positive results.

BENEFITS AND DOWNSIDES OF TEAM CONFLICT RESOLUTION SKILLS

You and your team have everything to gain by dealing with conflict in a healthy manner. There is no inherent downside to improved conflict resolution skills. However, it can be counterproductive if your team relies on one style exclusively. Too much of the same technique is boring and leads to complacency, which means that key matters could be mishandled or missed completely. Also be careful that you don't get caught up in discussing, processing, and analyzing things to death at the expense of getting the real work done.

DECISION MAKING AND THE HUMAN BRAIN

Individual and group decision making is at the heart of handling conflict well. We'll bet you've heard the injunction at a team meeting, "We have an important decision to make here, so leave emotions out of it." There's only one good response to that: "Impossible!" Humans just aren't wired that way. Emotions will always be intertwined with our logical reasoning. Our brain's limbic system, including the amygdala, plays a consistent role in our thinking because new information goes through the limbic system before it gets to our rational thinking center, known as the executive center. The executive center is our prefrontal cortex, the center for logical reasoning. Bar-On and his colleagues (2003) conducted research to confirm that our emotional and social decisions are unrelated to IQ. They evaluated patients who had deficits in emotional signaling because of lesions to the amygdala and related areas. These people had "severe impairment . . . in real-life decision-making and an inability to cope effectively with environmental and social demands" (p. 1790).

The brain-damaged patients were compared to a group without brain damage. Both were given IQ tests, the Bar-On EQ-i, and other measures. The researchers found no difference in IQ but big differences in the emotional and social intelligence skills of the patients. Their ESI scores were lower. Self-regard and assertiveness were the most affected competencies. People with damage to this critical part of the brain have trouble being aware of themselves and their emotions, understanding how to control their emotions, adapting to change, and solving problems.

For those of us who are blessed with healthy brains, the challenge is to learn to integrate all the parts of our brain for making good decisions for ourselves and our teams.

Even with a healthy brain, negative emotions, such as anxiety, interfere with the ability to think well. Amy Arnsten, director of graduate studies at the Yale University School of Medicine, wrote an article titled "The Biology of Being Frazzled" (1998) that explained scientifically something you have probably experienced yourself. When you're even mildly upset, your thinking becomes somewhat clouded. Your higher-order thinking becomes impaired.

As Daniel Goleman (2006) describes it, "frazzle is a neural state in which emotional upsurges hamper the working of the executive center of the brain" (p. 268). Organizational leaders have been teaching for years that fear doesn't work as an effective motivator. In fact, it shuts down some of our best thinking. Teams should take into account that choosing to evoke any particular emotion is a crucial strategic decision. Goleman continues, "The greater the anxiety we feel, the more impaired is the brain's cognitive efficiency. In this zone of mental misery, distracting thoughts hijack our attention and squeeze our cognitive resources. Because high anxiety shrinks the space available to our attention, it undermines our very capacity to take in new information, let alone generate fresh ideas" (p. 268).

ANGER AND OTHER NEGATIVE EMOTIONS

Anxiety isn't the only negative emotion affecting teams. Negative emotions are triggered by any number of factors, including these:

- *Values.* When team members hold deeply different beliefs about what is right, challenges can get nasty.
- *Power.* An inappropriate use of power occurs when one person or a clique seeks to make others do their bidding and does so without authority or without exercising respect for others. Power battles come in obvious as well as hidden ways and are one of the biggest factors diminishing a team's well-being and productivity.
- *Inequity.* This is the sense that fairness is violated because one person gets more than another or because your team isn't getting a fair shake.
- *Thwarted effectiveness.* Just like individuals, teams need to have pride in the outcome of their work. When they can't get their work done well, negative emotions are likely to follow.

Negative emotions grow in a progression that affects teams' effectiveness. The strategy needed to respond requires progressively more skilled and firmer responses from the team leader, teammates, and potentially the organization. We see it as the cascading effect depicted by our continuum of negative emotions (see Figure 8.1).

Anger is the negative emotion that most consistently threatens teams. When a team member is suddenly seething, screaming, or pounding the table, everyone gets quiet. Other teammates look at the floor or shuffle their feet. Most of the time, people don't know what to do with their discomfort. Generally, people would prefer to minimize or ignore the anger if possible. This avoidance will backfire—after all, there's an elephant in the room! Anger needs to be addressed with finesse.

Anger has a reputation, so let's put it in perspective. First, Gibson and Tulgan (2002) defined anger well as "a normal, basic emotion that ranges from mild irritation to intense rage. Like fear, anger stems from our instinct for self-preservation and is always provoked by some stimulus" (p. 3).

Three key questions are of paramount importance for teams:

1. How do we manage the environment so that emotions don't get out of hand?
2. How does each teammate handle his or her own anger?
3. How do you and your teammates respond to anger when it arises?

There are countless resources on understanding and managing anger. If this is a big concern for your team, get help from your employee assistance network, human resources, or an outside

FIGURE 8.1. THE CONTINUUM OF NEGATIVE EMOTIONS.

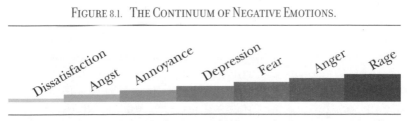

facilitator. Get some training—perhaps the team can take a course or a seminar on how to communicate or improve their conflict resolution skills. Remember to practice what you're taught!

Thich Nhat Hanh has every reason to know about anger. He's a Buddhist monk from Vietnam who has survived three wars and more than thirty years in exile. His book, simply titled *Anger* (2001), contains many wise strategies. One unexpected strategy is to give a gift, or at least the benefit of the doubt, to the one whom you feel anger toward. Yikes! That's more than a little gracious, yet the act of reaching out with genuine good intentions can transform the relationship. If you're stuck in a really angry conflict with a teammate, ask yourself if there's some gift that would show you really do understand the person. If so, give it (without expectation), and see what happens.

Should your safety be threatened because of bullying behavior, get help at once. Violence in the workplace happens. Too often people want to believe the anger is not that serious, but the truth is, avoidance can be dangerous. Be careful and proactive. You have a right to feel safe and secure in your workplace, and the people who lead it are responsible for providing that sense of basic safety.

EVOLUTIONARY CONFLICT: DIFFERENT WORLDVIEWS

Thomas Friedman, the *New York Times* foreign affairs columnist and Pulitzer Prize winner, toured a Lexus factory in Japan in 1992. He subsequently wrote a book called *The Lexus and the Olive Tree* (1999) in which he describes his experience of being struck by the robots that put the luxury cars together. That evening, as he ate sushi on a Japanese bullet train, he read a story about yet another Middle East squabble between Palestinians and Israelis. He reflected on the frequent and heated conflicts in the Middle East over who owns a particular olive tree. Friedman pondered the dramatic dichotomy: while half of the world was lusting after a Lexus or the brilliant technology that made such a machine possible, the other half was fighting over a single olive tree.

What does this have to do with the emotional and social functioning of your team? Plenty! Globalization is the fodder for abundant conflict within teams. The impacts can be direct: if your team function gets outsourced overseas, that will seriously disrupt the team. Or it could be an indirect impact: there might be increased expectations on your team if your organization is expanding into new markets. Pricing and competition may wreak havoc on your productivity numbers.

Furthermore, many teams are now spread out in multiple geographical locations; they might be in different parts of a city, of a country, or in several nations. If this is your team, just how will you forge allegiances and develop strong enough bonds to resolve a conflict when the next one arises? If you think conflict won't happen, you're deluding yourself. Not only can you count on it happening; count on it happening regularly. The business pressures are too enormous and the pace of innovation is too fast for conflict not to be part of your business mix. Conflict is common at the interface where change disrupts past success.

Deliberately and thoughtfully investing in building your team's emotional and social intelligence is essential for the team members to have the capacity to meet these challenges. We've said it before, and it bears repeating: broadening your perspective through increased awareness is a key element to team success.

In their illuminating book *The Cultural Creatives* (2000), Paul Ray and Sherry Ruth Anderson talk of three Americas. They are referring to three types of perspectives based in core values of what is right and wrong that separate our views in America. They call these three groups the traditionalists, the moderns, and the cultural creatives. The moderns make up about half of U.S. society, and the traditionalists and cultural creatives each have about one-quarter of the population. The perspectives held by these groups are radically different at times and are directly responsible for the "red state–blue state" split in recent U.S. voting patterns. The traditionalists, true to their name, believe that men and women should keep to their traditional roles; women are expected in large part to follow the decisions of men, and sexuality should be ruled by the church.

Moderns dominate society and are primarily responsible for the reporting by all major news media, such as *USA Today*,

Business Week, and the large television networks. They generally want to maintain the status quo and believe unquestioningly in the technological economy.

Cultural creatives are intrigued with authenticity, worldwide relationships, the economy, and women's issues. Self-actualization is much more important to this group than to the other two.

You can see that extremely different values and worldviews are held by these three groups. The value clusters that organize human behavior are given a finer description and much more pointed recognition of differences through a system known as Spiral Dynamics, described by Beck and Cowan (1996) and then taken to a much more explicit level by Don Beck in the system known as Spiral Dynamics Integral, which you can learn more about at http://www.spiraldynamics.net. Marcia has described both of these systems in more depth in her book *Life's 2% Solution* (Hughes, 2006). Whether you take time to study these different approaches or not, you cannot avoid dealing with the values issues they reflect. They show up in your team meetings. In the rare cases when a team is wholly composed of members of only one group, it creates an unrealistic and unbalanced scenario lacking diversity and customer representation. If you understand the differences well enough to work with them, you've got a strong and creative team that will be more in touch with your customer base and able to make the most of employee diversity within your organization.

Let's imagine we're looking in on the U.S. House of Representatives. This is the team of 435 members, a majority of whom voted in favor of legislation to allow increases in stem cell research. During the debate, you can be sure that all three points of view were proclaimed. Representatives from the traditionalist perspective might say, "No more research. It's unethical to play around with life; it should be left to God." The modernists might say, "Look, it's straight science, what can be wrong with that? Besides, scientists around the globe are doing it, and we'll lose our competitive edge, which will cost American businesses greatly." The cultural creatives might say, "Now is our chance to come together for the greater good of humanity. We can honor the metavalues of universal religious or spiritual beliefs while we provide inexpensive ways to help people dying unnecessarily of diseases in less developed countries."

At the bottom line, these different perspectives arise out of the differences in what individuals see as true and valuable. It's interesting that in a three-hour House debate on the legislation in January 2007, lawmakers cited Catholic theologian Thomas Aquinas, Paul the Apostle, Galileo, the Reverend Martin Luther King Jr., and the nation's founders in their arguments for removing President Bush's restrictions on stem cell research.

TIPS FOR GROWING YOUR CONFLICT RESOLUTION SKILLS

The emotions aren't always immediately subject to reason, but they are always immediately subject to action.
WILLIAM JAMES

- When a team member starts demonstrating emotions, such as annoyance or frustration, attend to it at the time rather than letting the negativity grow. Follow these guidelines:
  1. *Notice with respect.* Say something such as, "Jenny, you seem annoyed (or withdrawn or frustrated) by the tempo of our discussion. Is it the level of detail that doesn't work for you?"
  2. *Wait and listen for an answer.* Let the other person consider the question. We're often slow at being willing to be silent.
  3. *Find a way to address the concern.* For example, you could say, "You want to get the show on the road; you're tired of talking about it. Yet others don't feel ready yet. Let's budget the remaining time for our discussion so we can all know when we will move on.
- Learn which of the five conflict resolution styles you most prefer—avoiding, accommodating, compromising, competing, or collaborating. Expand your skills so that you sometimes use one of your least preferred strategies. At least three times a week, consciously apply one of those skills, and make a note of how it worked for you.
- Be patient and reflective in using empathic assertiveness with someone who feels angry. As long as the person is not threatening or intimidating someone personally, give your teammate the opportunity to vent his or her emotions. The person is

angry because the intention to accomplish something is being thwarted—trying to put a lid on the anger will only make things worse. Recognize the person's concern, and show respect. This does not require that you agree with the person! Just show empathy—the ability to reflect understanding and concern. However, don't leave it there. Be assertive about the need to resolve the concern so that the anger doesn't bring down your team. The team should work on specifics of who does what and when to build a resolution rather than sweeping the anger under the rug.

Taking the time to examine and enrich your skill set for resolving conflict will undoubtedly increase your self-confidence and your own authenticity. You'll already be enhancing your optimism, even before you start reading the next chapter!

CHAPTER NINE

THE SEVENTH SKILL: POSITIVE MOOD

You're only given a little spark of madness.
You mustn't lose it.
ROBIN WILLIAMS

His Holiness the Dalai Lama leads a big team—the Tibetan people. Tenzin Gyatso is the fourteenth Dalai Lama, and as such, he is the leader of Tibetan Buddhism and the exiled head of the outlawed Tibetan government. In both the Western and Eastern cultures, he is revered as a remarkable spiritual leader. His teachings and his ongoing compassion transcend religion. Although the Tibetan people have lived in conflict with the Chinese effort to take over their land since the 1950s, it would be difficult to find a leader who is more optimistic than the Dalai Lama. Think about that: his country has been taken over by a foreign government, he himself is persona non grata in his homeland, and yet he works tirelessly to care for Tibetan refugees all over the world, setting up schools and cultural centers to perpetuate and promote Tibetan culture, and he speaks with respect and compassion for the oppressors who have treated him, his country, and his people with such brutality. His optimism is unparalleled.

When you recall that emotions are contagious, you realize that the profound effect this leader's optimism has on his team—the Tibetan people—and the rest of world is incalculable. The positive attitude he displays with such integrity and sincerity provides hope to millions and shines as a role model for millions more. In the introduction to the Dalai Lama's book *Essential Teachings* (1995), Andrew Harvey wrote, "When the Dalai Lama laughs, it sounds as if all the other thirteen Dalai Lamas are laughing with him" (p. xiv).

WHAT POSITIVE MOOD IS FOR TEAMS

Optimism and happiness are both aspects of positive mood and are vital parts of emotional and social intelligence. Put simply, happiness is your ability to be satisfied with today. It reflects your ability to accept all that is here right now, embrace it, and be deeply grateful. The other part of your mood is your optimism, which is your hopefulness about future outcomes. It's reflected in a team's can-do attitude.

Believe it or not, team members deeply focused on their achievements may easily miss experiencing happiness today. You might think that the intense drive to the finish line would be a pure asset, but it's not the case. Serious athletes, even when they know they have done their best, still hope and intend to do even better next time. They are cautious about being satisfied for too long because they don't want to become complacent and lose their edge. However, they know that focusing exclusively on the future is overrated. There is something to be said for happiness in the moment and the energy it brings!

Many people, including the Dalai Lama, believe that the primary motivator in our lives is seeking happiness. If that's the case, it is of profound significance to teams. In his book *The Art of Happiness* (Dalai Lama and Cutler, 1998), the Dalai Lama says, "I believe that the very purpose of our life is to seek happiness. That is clear. Whether one believes in religion or not, whether one believes in this religion or that religion, we all are seeking something better in life. So, I think the very motion of our life is towards happiness" (p. 3).

You might think to yourself, "I'm not on this team to be happy; I'm here to support my family." The source of happiness for you is supporting your family. It might not be the work on the team per se but what it allows. But imagine what a better life you'd have if you were *both* happy working on the team and happy that it allowed you to support your family. Imagine how much happier your contagious emotions might help your family be.

Optimism is the fulcrum that balances satisfaction with today, on one side, and a belief that positive results are coming, on the other side. A colleague at a major insurance company recently told us that the insurer did research that demonstrated a very high correlation between optimism and success among its sales staff. This finding has led the company to decide that the price of admission to be hired at their company is optimism. People in sales get turned down, ignored, pushed away, and hung up on—how do they keep doing their job? Their tenacity has to be rooted in a strongly held belief that even though today didn't yield a sale, tomorrow is a new day. The salesperson stays positive with this self-message: "They'll be ready to buy tomorrow or on their next visit. Today, we built bridges in our relationship and to the product."

Martin Seligman, past president of the American Psychological Association, is the best-selling author of *Learned Optimism* (1991) and *Authentic Happiness* (2002). He is a founder of the field of positive psychology, which includes the study of positive emotions, character traits, and institutions. "'When pessimistic people run into obstacles in the workplace, in relationships, or in sports, they give up,'" he says. "'When optimistic people encounter obstacles, they try harder. They go the extra mile'" (Row, 1998).

People with a positive mood hang in longer when there's a challenge; they persevere. They also live longer and healthier lives and are more influential at work. These are considerable assertions, and they are backed up by science and solid organizational research cited in places such as Seligman's and Goleman's books. Furthermore, we suspect that you know that a positive mood is good for you just from your common sense: Whom would you rather have as your team leader, a happy person or a disgruntled one?

This isn't rocket science. But the impact may be skyrocketing when you realize that there is no reason to feel condemned to a negative, pessimistic attitude. Seligman (1991) identified three aspects that directly affect whether one is optimistic or pessimistic. He noted that the extent to which you assign permanence, pervasiveness, and personalization to things that happen has a direct effect on your state of mind. Based on our experience, he hit the nail on the head.

You and your team can decide to be more positive and then apply the guidance in Table 9.1 and the associated explanations in choosing how you characterize an event. In many areas, your language controls the quality of life you experience. Your choices in how you frame events in your life make a difference in every part of your life.

1. What sort of frequency do you attribute to the occurrence of good and bad things in your life? Your interpretation of life's events is critical to your sense of power. Here's a switch: be intentionally inconsistent! If something good happens, believe it's just normal—have a permanently positive interpretation. Believe that good things *always* happen to your team. If something bad happens, isolate it. Talk about it as a single, unusual event. "Our team missed our numbers this month, but there's still the rest of the quarter."

2. Narrow the scope of effect or breadth you give to explanations by being specific. If something bad happens, have a precise explanation for what happened so that you know where you went wrong and what you must change. A team with lower optimism would say, "Things just happened; we don't know why we were passed over when they assigned the new projects." A team with higher optimism finds specific reasons for events that affect the team. "We received the new project because we developed an outstanding proposal with specific deliverables." Or when things don't go as desired, "We didn't get the project because our price was too high, and we can see in retrospect that we didn't take the time to develop our fact statement sufficiently."

3. Temper your attitude when examining why bad things happen. Take appropriate responsibility for what happens so that you can feel in control of a situation, but not to the detriment of your self-esteem. If your team perceives itself as a victim of circumstances, you and your organization are in trouble. The language the team uses and the mood it invokes is crucial to the team's success. "We can take charge here. There are actions we can take to mitigate this time crunch. Let's parcel

TABLE 9.1. OPTIMISM AND YOUR WORDS.

(1) Frequency	(2) Breadth	(3) Attitude
Often Versus Infrequent	Specific Versus General ("Black Hole")	Responsible Party Versus Victim
Higher Optimism		
• **Good things** *always* **happen to me.** • **Bad things are rare.**	**"I know why this happened, and I can avoid it."**	**"I'm responsible."**
"My boss gave me a bonus; it's so great that I'm regularly acknowledged for my work."	"I got a flat tire because it's been three months since I checked the air in my tires or had them rotated."	"I can take action to change situations if I want."
"Whew, this project is late by two hours."		"I know what I did to trigger this response."
Lower Optimism		
• **Bad things** *always* **happen to me.** • **Good things are rare.**	**"Things just happen."**	**"I'm just a victim of the world I see."**
"This project is late; we never get things done on time."	"I got a flat tire. Things like that happen to me."	"I'm just unlucky."
"My boss complimented my work. What a fluke! That won't happen again."		"Bad things normally happen to me."

out our commitments and buy some time from clients with whom we have a good relationship. They'll trust us to deliver one week later." These powerful optimistic statements are quite different from "Oh, well, we just have to work around the clock. We were told to do it, and no one cares about what it means to us or our families."

THE SEVEN INGREDIENTS OF A POSITIVE TEAM MOOD

Seven characteristics are indicative of the skills that support a positive mood. As with the other skills, we encourage you to nurture these characteristics as your personal circumstances allow. This reflects a life journey, not a race to win today.

1. *Positive can-do attitude.* This needs no explanation, but an example might inspire you. Isabelle was just not going to be thwarted. She told the team she'd find research demonstrating the value of the company's new insurance plan, and she was determined to do so. She'd tried their normal research sources and found little relevant information; now she was riding the Metro to the Library of Congress. Just as she was telling herself how lucky she is to live in Washington, D.C., where there are such phenomenal libraries, she remembered Sean, the lobbyist she'd recently met from a national insurers' association. She got off the Metro and phoned him. Sean said he had just received some compelling new research that might be exactly what she was seeking and invited her to come to his office, a few blocks away. Isabelle thanked him and said, "I'll be right there."

Isabelle embodies the essence of a can-do attitude. She combines her upbeat belief that what she needs will work out with her willingness to work hard. That makes her a great asset for her team. Positive attitudes enhance brain functioning; they help us think more broadly and creatively, leading to more effective decisions.

If your team doesn't have a winning attitude right now, it can be changed. It requires that you make a decision to be more positive and that you intentionally establish a practice of making and reinforcing positive statements on a regular basis. Reward people who make positive statements with compliments like "I never thought of it that way" or "That gets me motivated to tackle this again." The reward doesn't have to be a tangible item. A smile of acknowledgment, a positive nod, a verbal compliment—these all provide powerful encouragement. For the team's benefit, try following up someone else's positive comment with one of your own. Margaret may say, "This is a mighty tight deadline, but we have gotten through this kind of a crunch before." Then you can say, "Yes, we have, and we can ask Timothy and his team to lend us some technical support—we've helped them out before."

2. *Hopefulness.* Emily Dickinson wrote, "Hope is the thing with feathers / That perches in the soul / And sings the tune without the words / And never stops at all." What a powerfully transformative attitude! Try bringing that frame of mind to team meetings. You'll be a breath of fresh air and a hopeful voice that can boost the entire team's spirit. Notice whether your team supports a hopeful outlook or just quickly dismisses hopeful comments as unrealistic. The more hopeful a team is, the greater its likelihood of success.

3. *Curiosity.* A positive mood allows you to be curious, and curiosity builds a sense of possibility. It is surprisingly helpful in getting you out of sticky situations too. Treat the trying situation as a puzzle. Perhaps you can suspend reality for a bit, forget what will happen if you don't deliver your widgets or annual report on time, and just move the pieces around to see what else is possible. When you temporarily suspend the constraining reality, you might find a surprising possibility. And the companion of curiosity is open-mindedness: the willingness to consider new ideas is an essential part of creating opportunities.

4. *Long-term view.* Optimism enables you to look down the road with positive, hopeful expectations for the future, regardless of whether you are happy today. You might be planning for tomorrow, next month, or ten years from now. The optimistic focus acknowledges that although things may be challenging now, work or luck or perseverance will help you achieve what you desire. It might be that the salesperson makes the sale, the lawyer wins the case, or you get the promotion you need to support your family. A long-term view is a required component of meeting today's challenges in a way that keeps you creative and committed.

5. *Attitude of abundance.* Team members' ability to see opportunities is affected by whether they see themselves as rich or poor, or as lacking what they need or having plenty. Feeling abundant

leads to a sense of possibility and creativity. If the team's core belief is that there is plenty, team members won't be thrown when something is in short supply—they'll find a way to work around it. Making the assumption of abundance will help your team manage all situations, easy or tough.

6. *Playfulness.* "Whistle while you work" isn't bad advice. Go ahead and shock folks; what the heck! Take time as a team to play. Many teams believe that having a good time means going out to the local pub after work. That may work for some, but there are many other ways to be playful right on the job. Do fun things. For example, bring everyone an unfolding whistle like kids have at parties, place it at their seats before a meeting starts, and see how long it takes before you start hearing tweets. Who says you're not supposed to have fun at work? Acting "grown up" isn't all it's cracked up to be. If anyone asks, explain that playful people are more creative and more likely to find better answers to challenges. And the brief moment of fun reduces tension, and that saves everyone time and money by lowering stress. That's your business case for being playful; it helps the bottom line. Skip with it!

7. *Zest.* A team acting with zest exudes energy, has a positive sense of urgency, and remains focused on the team's purpose. Members are seldom caught making excuses or acting bored. Your showing zest or enthusiasm for your work will inspire your team. Teams have to believe that their mission has meaning and that they are making a worthwhile contribution. There's a complementary relationship between a positive mood and zest—each expands the other—to the benefit of your team. Similarly, a team with a positive mood is likely a motivated and enthusiastic team. These skills go hand in hand.

WHY TEAMS NEED A POSITIVE MOOD

Here's a team for you: more than six hundred crew members and volunteers from local service providers in Colorado's Jefferson County who in 2004 teamed up with ABC-TV crews from the show *Extreme Makeover: Home Edition* to build a two-family house in record time. And not just any two-family house; this one has revolving

doors, figuratively speaking: it is intended to hold two new families every two years. The 2,200-foot house provides shelter for two
families who find themselves homeless, out of work, or significantly
underemployed and have the initiative to want to help themselves
and realize their life goals. The families have to have a vibrant
hope that things will get better to be chosen to live in this house.

For example, Frankie, the head of one of the first two families
to move in, lost a succession of jobs due to corporate downsizing.
At the time his family was selected, he was earning a mere $5.00
an hour—not enough to pay for housing for his family. But
Frankie kept trying. Tim Little, division president of Standard
Pacific Homes, reported that he and his crew learned a lot about
the homeless in their marathon week of building. "These people
had jobs," he said. Homelessness, he learned, is "not always about
drugs and alcohol" and has a disastrous effect on the working
poor and their children (Wheeler, 2004).

The magic of *Extreme Makeover* projects is that the new or
rebuilt home is created in just one week. To build the Colorado
house, shifts of 125 people worked around the clock, and when
construction was finished, separate designer teams came in to
work wonders on the interior, from furnishings to toothbrushes.
If you've seen this ABC show, you know that despite the grueling
schedule, the workers have fun, and that's not a surprise, as all the
ingredients are present—motivated people, high visibility, ample
funding, local support—and they know their work has enormous
meaning for both the families and the entire community. That
new home provides the sense of security necessary to regenerate
self-respect, motivation, and the positive attitude it takes for the
beneficiary families to rebuild and significantly improve their
lives. It is also a focus for rebuilding community spirit and civic
participation.

Two local nonprofits helped find and support the first two
families who moved into the house. We work with one of the nonprofits, Jeffco Action Center, so we had an inside view of the great
numbers of teams it took to make these two new homes a reality.
The teams included the families, the nonprofits, the neighborhood volunteers, the two builders involved and all their crews, the
ABC *Extreme Makeover* crew, the local governments who helped

move the permitting through at lightning speed, and we're sure the list goes on. All of these teams became one complex, cross-functional, cohesive team willing and able to do whatever it took to get the job done.

This inspiring story demonstrates the use of all seven ingredients to create highly effective teams with positive moods. Some people challenge us on the whole notion of a positive mood. They say it's a nice extra, but it's just not important when there's a lot to get done. When we can, we show them pictures of the crews working on the *Extreme Makeover* house. What's more solid than the result of this team's work: a whole building constructed in just seven days? Positive attitude is crucial whenever teams need to get a lot done in a hurry.

BENEFITS AND DOWNSIDES OF A POSITIVE MOOD

Combine a highly optimistic team that is excited about the numerous possibilities it can think of to make contributions, add low doses of reality testing, and you have the makings of an overworked team. Reality testing, the skill of recognizing and responding to what is actually happening rather than a personal hallucination, helps remind us all of the great equalizer: no matter who you are, you have twenty-four hours in the day. You can use those hours optimistically, but you can't expand them. When you combine positive mood with reality testing, you are more able to not take on too much. If team members get carried away with all they theoretically can do, they may take on too much and find themselves working when they should be with their families or fulfilling personal goals. They may also find that quality suffers in favor of quantity. Balance is the key to not becoming so overloaded by your can-do attitude that you burn out or alienate your family.

BUILDING ON YOUR STRENGTHS

Your team strengths are the things you do best—they are your assets. Build on them, and you'll all be happier. Sometimes our attention can get fixated on our weaknesses and lead us to spend precious resources to improve those just a little instead of employing our natural strengths and talents. Although overcoming weaknesses can be a noble goal (and sometimes a necessary one), research has consistently demonstrated that we are much more likely to be successful, happy, and productive when we're working from our strengths. Imagine asking your sales team to take over the job for the information technology department. It makes you shudder to think of it! It's a really bad idea. Similarly, you don't want the quiet, technically oriented IT folks being in charge of promoting your products. Individuals and teams have areas where they excel and areas that just aren't right for them.

Two major strategies for understanding your strengths predominate in the workplace. One comes from the Gallup Organization and is described in *Now, Discover Your Strengths* (2001) by Marcus Buckingham and Donald Clifton. They discuss strengths as things that you are nearly perfect at—think of Tiger Woods playing golf or Julia Child cooking. Gallup's core question is one every team should seek to answer positively: Does your job allow you every day to do what you do best? If it doesn't, explore what you can do to make it a better fit.

The other popular approach is presented by the Values in Action Institute and explained by Martin Seligman in *Authentic Happiness* (2002). This approach is based on developing universally identified virtues, such as wisdom, courage, and justice, that naturally support our application of our strengths. The institute's twenty-four signature strengths include open-mindedness, curiosity, zest, and ingenuity. In fact, many of those strengths parallel the ingredients to create and sustain a positive mood. Given that the purpose of this book is expanding emotional and social intelligence in teams, it is interesting to notice that the fifth strength on the institute's list is social intelligence. One who excels in this skill, Seligman reports, "is aware of the motives and feelings of others, and . . . can respond well to them. Social intelligence is the ability to notice difference among others, especially with respect to their moods, temperament, motivations, and intentions—and then to act upon these distinctions" (pp. 143–144). Mahatma Gandhi reportedly pointed out that "there is more to life than increasing its speed." Sometimes increasing its quality *will* require the hard work and the persistent disciplined attention necessary to improve the social and emotional intelligences in which you are deficient.

In *Life's 2% Solution* (Hughes, 2006), Marcia guides her readers to work with their strengths in order to experience authentic success. We have the same advice for teams. To perform with authentic success as a team, you need a consensus of values and motivation so that you're working cohesively. This core foundation is then complemented by focusing your energies and output to accomplishing results by using your strengths. You will find differences in strengths among your team members; try to balance those differences to strengthen your connections with each other and to support your ability to understand other teams or colleagues. As you develop your team, seek out projects that maximize your strengths. If you don't have that much flexibility, take stock of what you're good at and what you most enjoy doing at work, and see if you can use those approaches as you accomplish your assigned work.

FRIENDS AT WORK

Some strategies for improving teams are easy to understand even though they may take some effort. Here's an excellent one: develop a good friend at work. In *Vital Friends* (2006), Tom Rath reports on research that shows that employees' satisfaction increases by almost 50 percent if they have close friendships at work. Loyalty, trust, and high energy are attributes universally desired of teams. Having valued relationships at work helps each of those qualities develop and mature.

Connections give us energy, and there's a marked difference between your connections with a team member you just barely know and your connection with a good friend. A good friend at work is someone you can count on, someone who "has your back." That friend will protect and support you if you're being gossiped about, challenged, or tested. When you're beleaguered, that's the kind of person you want on your team. Who on your team has your back? It's an important question; you'll be able to operate more flexibly and take more risks if you feel you have people who will look out for you. Those people are called friends, and having even one good friend on your team as an ally can make the work of improving its collective ESI a much smaller and easier job.

FINDING YOUR COMPETITIVE EDGE

In her work on mood contagion in groups, Barsade (2002) cites many sources showing that the existence of positive feelings in groups has consistently been shown to lead to more helpful and cooperative behavior. In negotiations, people in positive moods are more cooperative; salespeople in positive moods are more helpful when working with customers.

Not surprisingly, conflict is more often associated with negative moods. Negative moods diminish team cohesion and the sharing of the team workload. All of this emphasizes the importance of managing your team's moods. Fortunately, Barsade's research as well as that of others shows that positive mood spreads more readily than negative mood and so it has a greater effect—it is more "contagious." Furthermore, the emotions we pick up from one another also influence subsequent group dynamics.

Because teammates will pick up and mimic one another's moods, we encourage you to manage your own mood to accentuate the positive. Some of the benefits you'll enjoy include living a more exciting and fulfilling life, being generally healthier, and being likely to achieve more of the goals you desire. Certainly, in an age of cynicism and antidepressants, a positive mood will give you a competitive edge!

TRANSCENDENT VALUES

Dan Pink, author of *A Whole New Mind* (2005), presents a compelling argument that our world has changed irrevocably. The globalized information explosion, omnipresent media marketing, and a radical relocation of the manufacturing base mean that your team must add unique value if it is going to maintain its competitive edge. In and of itself, another new product will never get noticed in a market flooded with physical abundance. Imbue what you do with your own positive mood! Find a way to make your product or service *feel* optimistic and encouraging.

Pink emphasizes the importance of taking your results to a level that creates more than material satisfaction. His work comports with our findings. As people's material needs are increasingly satisfied, the higher self-actualization needs from Maslow's hierarchy begin to draw them with a more transcendent motivation. A positive mood supports teams and individuals in their pursuit of a higher purpose. It fosters the notion that one person and one team can make a substantial, meaningful, and lasting contribution to the world. A positive mood can capture the imagination and the hearts of team members and help them find personal meaning. Think of the results of the *Extreme Makeover* team creating two homes for formerly homeless families.

Tips for Growing Your Team's Positive Mood

- Follow the Dalai Lama's advice as you make team decisions; frame your decisions with the question, "Will this bring us and our customers greater happiness?" Be sure you are focusing on true long-term happiness, not fleeting pleasure.
- Honor the spirit of playfulness. Surprise your team, bring toys to work, or cut out relevant cartoons and pass one around at the start of each meeting. Celebrate your diversity by having a potluck lunch where everyone cooks a favorite dish, or create contests between different teams at work and offer fun prizes such as a professional chair massage at work. Play high-energy oldies from various decades during morning and afternoon breaks. Having fun does not have to be expensive.
- If your team is overwhelmed by a particular challenge, stop trying to solve it for an hour. Devote that hour to no-limits brainstorming on the topic. The first idea has to be kooky; after that, all possibilities are allowed. For the moment, no one can question them. Once you have a list of ideas, split into pairs, and give each pair one of those ideas. Each team must present its idea as if it's the best option. Act like you're certain that it's the best way to go, that it will be the answer for the long term, and that you have all the resources it takes to make this a success. You are likely to experience some interesting benefits. First, you're likely to have a sense of relief

just because the team lightened up. Second, you're much more likely to find a way around the big challenge. And third, engaging in these kinds of strategies will build team cohesiveness. If this doesn't help your team get creative and gain perspective, we suggest you call it a day!

PART THREE

RESULTS GAINED BY EMOTIONALLY AND SOCIALLY INTELLIGENT TEAMS

CHAPTER TEN

THE EMOTIONALLY INTELLIGENT TEAM PLAYER

The key elements in the art of working together are how to deal with change, how to deal with conflict, and how to reach our potential. . . . The needs of the team are best met when we meet the needs of individual persons.
MAX DEPREE

We wrote this book because we want you, the individual team member, to be able to use the seven skills of emotional and social intelligence and the techniques in this book to begin improving the working conditions on your team. It may take a while before you start to see progress, especially if you're all alone in your quest. But no one says you have to be! Maybe all the members of your team are not totally receptive to these ideas and eagerly awaiting the information so they can begin putting it to work right away, but even if you can recruit just one coconspirator, that's still a big step in the right direction! With enough persistence and flexibility, even if you're all alone you can use this material to improve the quality of your life at work—and that will matter to everyone on your team. This chapter includes specific techniques for improving each of the seven skills.

Some of the strategies you are likely to want include the ability to influence other team members when they are stuck or going off on an unproductive tangent. You may need to protect one team member who has become the emotional scapegoat. There will also be times when you need to be able to gracefully absorb the shocks that come your way when your colleagues are stressing out in general or not happy with *your* performance. The skills that make these kinds of midcourse corrections successful are ESI skills. They are what help teams develop the resilience everyone is talking about, the ability to bounce back from delays, upsets, and failures and become productive once again.

Let's get started with an example of how to work with other folks first. One of the primary skills lacking in the world of teamwork (and the world of work in general) is empathy. It turns out that empathy isn't something we have to wait for our colleagues to develop; it's something we can ask for and facilitate between team members. Empathy is a result of applying the seven core ESI skills.

Imagine that the following exchange is happening between you and a colleague:

Colleague: [*stopping you to raise this same issue for the third time*] Why can't you just get off the fence and decide to take the hit on that old inventory and get it out of here?

Emotionally: I know you've asked me this before. You really want
Intelligent me to make a decision right now! [*You match the*
You (EIY) *sense of urgency in your colleague's voice, which gives him the feedback that tells him you received both his verbal and nonverbal messages.*] Maybe if you knew how I feel about this, it would help us communicate more effectively. How do you think I feel?

Colleague: I don't know. If this is so important, why don't you just *tell* me how you feel?

EIY: I will, but humor me here. Understanding *your* perception of how I feel gives me the feedback I need to gauge how effectively I'm communicating with you.

Colleague: I think you're feeling smug. That's how you seem to me.

EIY: OK, tell me about that. You think I'm feeling smug because . . . [*Notice that you don't correct him, you just reflect what he said.*]

Colleague: I think you're feeling smug because the way this is playing out gives you all the control [*or*] I think you're feeling scared because you don't know what to do next [*or*] I think you're feeling angry because no one's getting you the data you need.

EIY: OK, this lets me know I'm not doing a very good job of communicating what I'm feeling. [*You always want to take responsibility for this because ultimately it is your responsibility and because even if your colleague is the least observant person in the world, criticizing him at this point will not help the two of you communicate better.*] I'm feeling very excited! I'm feeling excited because I've got a really hot lead, and they told me they'd get back to me by yesterday with an answer on how many units they want to buy. They didn't yet, but I'm not going to bug them until after lunch.

Colleague: Oh.

EIY: So how am I feeling?

Colleague: You feel excited.

EIY: That's right, I feel excited, because . . .

Colleague: You feel excited because you've got a hot lead that actually might get some of this inventory off our hands.

EIY: Exactly! I'm sorry I didn't do a better job in communicating that to you; I guess I've just been a little nervous. To heck with that, I'm going to go call him now! But first notice how I look, because this is excited. Once I sell him two hundred heat exchanger units, come look at me again—'cause then I'll look smug!

REQUESTING EMPATHY

This is a communication pattern we call "requesting empathy." Obviously, your specific communication may be significantly different from this, but any request for empathy means you are asking a team member to identify what you are feeling and why.

1. Start by giving reflective feedback that demonstrates you have heard what the other person is saying, and then ask what the person thinks *you* are feeling.

2. Gently and respectfully deflect any evasion the person might attempt. Say, "I'll tell you, but humor me first. Right now, understanding *your* perception of how I feel will tell me how easy it is to 'read' me. I hope I can make it clearer next time."

3. Whatever the person says, repeat it respectfully for confirmation: "You think I'm feeling . . ." This should be pretty simple, but if you get it wrong, the person will correct you. If your colleague tells you something different, simply reflect that. After a brief pause, add the word *because* with a questioning tonality that prompts the person to volunteer why he or she thinks you feel that way.

4. If the response is correct, acknowledge this positively. If the person doesn't or can't identify why you're feeling that way, respectfully explain what you *are* feeling instead.

5. Then elicit confirmation by saying, "So I'm feeling . . . ," and if the person doesn't add the meaning portion spontaneously ("because . . ."), give that cue again.

This kind of no-fault correction with targeted appreciation is what helps your team members learn how to give you what you want. It will be quite helpful if you can practice it with a friend a few times before you actually use it with your team. What's so neat is that *everyone* can benefit from this, whoever you might recruit to help you out—a spouse, a friend, a trusted colleague.

TAKING YOUR EMOTIONAL PULSE

Here's a technique you can use to improve your own effectiveness in the art of emotional communication. Use a slightly different version of the same pattern; this time it will be "I feel _____ because _____." You don't actually have to use the word *feel;* just state your emotion ("I'm happy, sad, frustrated, puzzled"). Now before you actually do this publicly, you need to be certain that you do know what you're feeling and why. (Otherwise, you could confuse everyone about how you look when you feel a certain way or, worse, unintentionally give them the impression that you are trying to mislead them.) This is using your skill of emotional awareness.

This territory is more familiar to some people than to others. Some of us grew up in homes where feelings were denied, ignored, or intentionally misrepresented. Some of us grew up in homes where it was absolutely essential to know what other people were feeling (perhaps in order to stay safe!). That will make you really good at empathy, but taking your *own* emotional pulse is a skill that requires paying attention *internally* so you can identify what *you* are feeling and why.

If this is unfamiliar territory for you, a great way to develop the skill is to chart your emotional pulse in a little notebook that you carry around with you. You'll need to take notes at least five or six times a day for two weeks. Initially, your emotional vocabulary may be clustered around the "mad, glad, sad" family, but over those two weeks, it will start to become increasingly more nuanced. You might hear yourself saying, "I feel perturbed" or "delighted" or "disappointed." Then you may begin making even finer distinctions: "miffed," "thrilled," "forlorn." There are more feeling words in the English language than in any other—no need to skimp! Make it a point to notice them when other people are speaking; look in the dictionary or in a thesaurus or under "feeling words" on the Internet. These words are powerful bridges that help the people in your life cross the gap between the behavior they see on the outside and what's happening inside your life.

You want the people on your team to understand the cognitive meaning of your communication, but you also need them to understand the *emotional value* that you place on what you are saying because you probably want them to feel the same way. Expanding your emotional vocabulary will help you give your messages the emotional highlighting necessary to make them stand out.

"At last we don't have to use that ridiculous SR-6 form when we file our expense reports anymore. I feel elated because that was the biggest waste of time in my day!" Now your team members can chime in with you and celebrate the procedural death of this dinosaur.

TELLING IT TO 'EM STRAIGHT

For some people, direct communication is a significant hurdle, even when discussing small matters. Team leader or not, you can help. Remember, you can change outcomes both by virtue of your position and by virtue of your influence. As a team member, you owe it to your colleagues to be sensitive while being direct. If you can assist others in being more direct, that's even better. Direct communication is particularly challenging when an issue is likely to be contentious. That's also the time when honest dialogue is most needed.

A friend of yours on the team named Sara is an introvert and is consistently quieter than the other members. She processes her thoughts and feelings longer than other team members because she prefers to build a more complete understanding before she speaks. That is not a problem, but when she does speak, Sara beats around the bush instead of saying what she really means or wants. You can generally figure out what she's trying to say, but you can't always take the time to decode her communications, and neither can your other teammates. This means your friend's opinion, which is often quite insightful, gets neglected at the cost of quality and productivity. Furthermore, she's marginalized, receives little respect from her teammates, and is losing self-regard.

You can help Sara learn to speak more assertively if you're willing to invest a little effort. Let's imagine she gives you a convoluted message to decode:

> Sara: Sometimes, when it's getting close to the end of the day and we have an order of sales kits to get out, I get a call from shipping wondering how soon they need to arrive, because by the time they get them to the post office, the priority mail may have already gone out. If any are especially time-sensitive, they want to know if they can send them overnight, which at that time of day means they'd be guaranteed second-day delivery. It costs about three times as much, around fifty-four dollars.

> Emotionally: It feels like you're asking me a question, and I'd
> Intelligent like to answer it, but I can't figure out precisely
> You (EIY) what you're asking. This happens often enough that I think the two of us could benefit from developing a work-around that gets to the point more directly.

Sara: Well, OK, I guess, if you think so, maybe we could figure something out.

EIY: Sometimes requests make people uncomfortable. I know you want to respect people's feelings by being polite, but when everybody's so busy, it's also important to respect their time. If you were more direct and less polite, I think it would help me work with you more effectively.

Sara: [*a little flustered*] Well, OK, I guess, if you think so.

EIY: Yes, I think so! [*A moderately strong affirmation at a moment when she feels hesitant can help her feel that you are comfortable with her being more assertive.*] We can have a code that lets me know you are going to speak less formally and cut to the chase. Then I won't feel like you're being impolite. [*It is very important for her not to feel that she is being impolite.*]

Sara: That would be good.

EIY: So how about if you started off by saying, "To respect your time . . ." before you tell me directly what it is you want or need? I'll recognize that as our code and expect you to speak less formally and more directly.

Sara: OK.

EIY: OK, good. Let's try it now. Give me the code, and then you can start over with your question about shipping.

Sara: To respect your time, when shipping calls toward the end of the day to ask if any packages need to go overnight, we need someone or some way to decide.

EIY: Great! That's enormously better! Now I understand the issue, but I still don't hear you asking for what I think you really need. Let's try one more time, and be downright blunt with me, please!

Sara: To respect your time, can I be the one to let shipping know which sales kits need to go overnight when the outgoing mail is going to be late?

EIY: Brilliant! That is so much more efficient and respectful! Of course, you're the one with the best information about this, so you should decide.

Obviously, you will have to modify these instructions for your own specific situation, but try to preserve as many of the language patterns as possible. For example, "To respect your time" both consciously holds your less assertive team member accountable for being direct *and* gets them off the hook for not being as polite as they probably feel they should be. It's amazing what a respectfully stated straight answer to a direct question does in a group. Immediately, trust goes up. So does respect. Part of the problem, of course, is getting your other team members to ask their questions directly. Applying your ESI skills, you can be the one to use your influence with everyone!

GAINING FLEXIBILITY

We could all use a little yoga—not just physically but mentally and emotionally too! Inflexibility is a typical challenge that can significantly affect a team's productivity. You or your team may get so caught up in following a form, process, or rule that your rigid adherence derails functionality. The principle that "form follows function" is a great mantra for life. Age and routine can contribute to declining flexibility. Most teenagers are prime examples of flexibility. They call home on a whim wanting to go out with friends, wanting to switch family plans at the last minute, wanting an extension on their curfew! They seek to respond to life's constant changes very spontaneously. Perhaps we could all learn a little from their flexibility.

However, before you plunge into making wholesale changes in the name of flexibility, pause for a minute. Remember, you have become who you are for a number of very good reasons. You didn't just turn out as you did on your own. Who you are right now is the direct result of all the experiences and learning that have occurred in your life thus far. You've been successful in many ways. Some things are working well for you now. Some aren't. The truth is that the present gets more and more unlike the past all the time, and the problems that your team has to solve will probably be increasingly different and require more innovative solutions. So one trick to use for increasing your flexibility is to help yourself feel more comfortable with change by changing gradually, but frequently, in little ways.

The ability to change is like a muscle, and for people who are low in flexibility, they use that muscle as little as possible. Changing is a generalized experience in human life—you might hurt your wrist and have to brush your teeth with your other hand, get a flat tire and have to change it, or have to alter the route you drive to work because of a construction project; these are all events that engage your change muscle. Like your physical muscles, your change muscle gives you the best service when you stretch it and exercise it regularly.

To begin your new change exercise program, change little things at first—fun things, even funny things! Put a note on the bathroom mirror that says "OTHER HAND" and the date. Start out brushing your teeth every day for two weeks with the "wrong" hand. Unless you actually keep at it till you learn how, it will take too long to do the whole job that way, and after a while, you are likely to change back to what's "normal." Keep at it and applaud yourself for starting your day by embracing change!

We can't emphasize this enough. Smile to yourself internally, wink at yourself in the mirror, and pat yourself on the back physically. By letting your unconscious mind know "This is what I want! This is important!" it will begin to help you change at a profound level you cannot reach in any other way. As we noted earlier in this book, your unconscious mind functions with the intelligence of a child who is around seven years old. It is very concrete, and when approached respectfully and patiently, it will begin to follow the instructions you give it to the best of its ability. Thank it in advance, encourage it, and praise it. It may sound goofy, but if you follow this strategy, you'll develop a relationship with this dynamic character within, giving you a significant advantage in your ability to accomplish behavioral change. The unconscious mind operates at the level where all the "old tapes" were recorded and are now stored. This is the only place where they can be changed.

TESTING REALITY

Research is all about exploration and discovery. It's also about affirming what you thought you knew in the first place. Anecdotal evidence may be confirmed or refuted by a quantitative study.

Testing reality is a form of research offering powerful ways to become a more effective team player. This practice confirms or denies how well your personal experience fits with the objective reality that everyone agrees on, more or less. It's the quickest way to determine whether you're in denial, wearing rose-colored glasses, or right on target.

If you are testing reality so intensely that you need to figure out what the worst-case scenario is for every project and relationship you are involved in, you're overdoing it. In that case, there isn't enough room left on your radar screen to notice the positive creative opportunities you can take advantage of to improve team life. If, on the other hand, the glasses that you're wearing are so rosy that you can barely see through them, you can expect to be blindsided or at least encounter unpleasant surprises on a pretty regular basis.

If you feel like you're getting too far removed from the more specific, measurable, concrete appreciation of life, you can quickly recalibrate your focus by asking other people, from their point of view, what the context and the significant variables are for the specific problem you are seeking to solve. Their point of view can serve as a barometer, a way to test the direction of the wind, a way to see the world differently and open your thinking to something new.

Sometimes it's worthwhile to figure out how to quantify and compare the issues you're considering. Maybe someone else has already developed a way to measure the results of the strategy your team is considering. If so, see if it will work for you. If not, consider setting up a system of record keeping to compare what the subject is like today with how it has been in the past.

Developing Team Relationships

Whereas most of the ESI skills are ones that individual team members benefit from developing on their own as well as at the team level, some aspects of team relationships can be undertaken by everybody on the team all at once. Such events as team-building retreats and team time-outs help foster healthy team relationships. Plan in advance, make a commitment, and go off-site when possible. This is about getting to know each other in ways that extend beyond the concerns and tasks of your work life together.

Anticipating how each other is likely to respond to challenges in the workplace requires knowing more about the deeper values and goals that organize the purposes of your individual lives. Build your team smarts with this kind of emotional literacy.

Telling stories about events that have happened in your past is an excellent way to build understanding. If money is available, a professional facilitator's skills and insights are often valuable; but if there are no funds for that assistance, don't let it stop you. Here are some examples of the kinds of stories that will begin building deeper levels of connection and trust within your team:

- Describe your favorite gift and what made it so special.
- Share your earliest memory of money.
- If you had to change one thing in the way you've lived your life, tell what it would be.
- Ponder whether growing up in a different geography would have changed you.
- Play charades or other "party games" that depend on communication and connecting.

Another way of relating to each other that can be exceptionally beneficial is to undertake some kind of a small construction project. Build something together in which you all have to follow the same instructions; the best such projects include subcomponents that groups of two or three can work on together and then bring back to the whole group.

Outdoor activities, even just taking a walk together for an hour or so, can help you begin to see and appreciate each other in a different context. The more you know each other, the easier it is to trust, and the more reason there is to do so. The real value of building team relationships is that when everyone understands more about how each of you became who you are, your quirks, your hot buttons, your strengths, your challenges, and your passions, it creates synergy and understanding and leads to better outcomes and best practices. It allows you to help each other compensate and respond with greater flexibility and resilience, turning the stress of change into creative opportunities where you rise to the occasion together. It is the birthplace of the extraordinary team.

GO FORTH AND COLLABORATE

Being a fully effective and fully participatory team member requires your ongoing commitment to the team's success. You have to be willing to take full responsibility for all of your own assignments and one share of the responsibility for team improvement. Some people have difficulty taking full responsibility for anything, and their lives typically show the lack of empowerment that such unwillingness creates. However, it they regularly observe you taking these kinds of risks and doing your best to fulfill them, their desire to achieve more of what they truly want may tempt them to think and act outside the box and follow that example. Your commitment to continue developing your emotional and social intelligence skills may be all the example that your team members need.

Team leadership is seldom easy, but it's even more difficult when a team intends to reach the multileader level of excellence at which the leadership can be shared according to who is best suited to lead the task currently at hand. Hopefully, you are or one day will be a member of such a team. Whenever average teams begin to excel and accomplish shared leadership, it is usually because in the difficult times, the voice of one emotionally intelligent team member called the others to remember their purpose, their successes, their desire and commitment to perform well together, and what they can accomplish when they do. We hope this chapter has given you some of the tools and encouragement to help you be that voice in those difficult moments and champion the full potential of your team!

CHAPTER ELEVEN

LEADING THE EMOTIONALLY INTELLIGENT TEAM

A lieutenant who commanded infantry troops in World War II was legendary for the success he had in the European theater. When it was time to attack, he was the first man out of the foxhole, leading his troops into battle every time. He was revered as a hero among his troops. His courage in the face of enemy fire was remarkable.

Not surprisingly, he was honored for his exceptional leadership. A ceremony was held at which he was awarded the Silver Star and the Purple Heart. After the general read the commendation for the lieutenant's repeated bravery and success at routing the enemy and personally pinned the medals on his chest, a newspaper reporter sought him out. He had one question. This man simply had to know why the lieutenant was always first into the fray of battle. After all, he was an officer, and being first was extremely hazardous.

The lieutenant, a man of few words, looked the reporter in the eye and asked, "Have you ever tried to push a string?"

ADAPTED FROM "LIFE IN THESE UNITED STATES," *READER'S DIGEST*, 1950s

Emotionally intelligent leadership is the practice of being what success in the current situation requires. Wherever team members are committed to achieving a clear vision of success and have that kind of example, they cannot fail if they do not quit! That's how ESI leadership builds and sustains organizational excellence. Research has repeatedly shown that successful leaders are highly skilled in these competencies, and that is what distinguishes the great from the good.

Leadership makes a tremendous difference in team performance. The leader, whether by position or by influence, can establish positive behavioral norms about how the team manages emotions and relationships. Through instructions and example, the leader can show team members how to be empathic, to be more aware of how they are perceived, to be savvy enough to understand the political landscape, and to be smart enough to get the resources and support they need. But it is the leader who must *be* authentic, collaborative, able to manage his or her own emotions and those of others, and able to deal with conflict effectively. In short, it takes high-level emotional and social intelligence. It also takes courage.

Courage is a core attribute defining ESI leaders. The degree to which you model courageous behavior influences your team's courage and commitment. It takes courage to navigate difficult conversations and issues with integrity. It takes courage to stay the course when the team is under stress or teetering on the edge of disaster and the necessary corrections are unpopular.

TRANSPARENCY

Transparency is a buzzword that resonates with consumers, employees, watchdog groups, political adversaries, and government entities in the quest for greater accountability. This same principle applies to leadership. Transparency in leadership means being intellectually honest and open so that people can read you. It means being emotionally aware and sharing that information, perhaps by taking your emotional pulse publicly on a regular basis. When talking about you, people will call you "reliable" and say, "What you see is what you get." Being transparent supports your team's emotional literacy because you provide sufficient data to read you accurately. That builds trust and demonstrates integrity and congruence. Team members know what to expect consistently. Sometimes transparency gets confused with humility and having a low sense of self-importance. Although these are important qualities for ESI leadership, here's how they differ.

Carlos Castaneda's mentor Don Juan taught his apprentices continuously about the hazards of self-importance. "Self-importance is man's greatest enemy. What weakens him is feeling offended by the deeds and misdeeds of his fellow man. Self-importance requires that one spend most of one's life feeling offended by something or someone" (1998, p. 230). Jim Collins identified personal humility as one of the critical factors for achieving great leadership. In *Good to Great* (2001), he points out that a great leader "acts with quiet, calm determination; relies principally on inspired standards to motivate, not inspiring charisma; and channels ambition into the company, not the self, setting up successors for even greater success in the next generation" (p. 38).

Transparency is different from humility inasmuch as it incorporates a sense of congruency with one's announced and unannounced principles and standards. Whereas humility emphasizes not claiming for yourself more than you are entitled to, transparency invites a kind of public accountability and a promise to be true to the values and behaviors expected of you.

In essence, it's our aptitude for trustworthiness. It requires significant skill in the emotional competency Reuven Bar-On (1997) calls social responsibility, which includes the ability to connect with people and to commit to your group or team. Trustworthiness includes not only self-awareness and self-management but also vision and inspirational leadership. When you thoughtfully consider the learning styles, values, and priorities of your team as a whole, you can generate commitment by crafting an emotionally resonant message. It requires big-picture thinking, out beyond the borders of personal self-concern. A great team is made up of people who intimately understand the needs and concerns of their internal and external customers and are motivated by both compassion *and* profit to meet as many of those needs as possible.

The transparency that is necessary for leading an emotionally intelligent team is even greater than that required for an average team. Emotionally intelligent teams have even higher standards of authenticity and are more assertive in communicating with their leaders.

This need not be intimidating; you can always improve your ESI skills, and a more skillful team will actually help you do so. One of the most effective ways of practicing transparency is to take your own emotional pulse in team meetings. Letting your team know what you are feeling and why can make a huge difference in motivating all its members. You can learn to emotionally highlight your message and incentivize your team to move toward or away from the behaviors you identify.

For example, imagine a marketing team seeking to offset the significant gains a competitor is making with a new point-of-purchase display. The market research company the team hired is providing very detailed information, but it's coming in so slowly that it's almost useless. One work-around is having the field send individual reports to the marketing team in real time. The marketing team would have to compile the reports but would have the data considerably faster. The team does not have the experience or the training to interpret customer behavior from the raw data yet; what it does have is the jitters. There are dozens of reasons why the team shouldn't take this approach and dozens of ways they could be coached to work with this raw data.

The team leader realizes that this is a stretch, but it's the only way to speed the data through the pipeline. It's up to the leader to move the team toward embracing this faster approach, but he knows it won't work if he just barks orders. He needs to communicate in a way that will generate acceptance and commitment. To mitigate resistance, he needs to connect on an emotional level, perhaps with empathy or humor. His own style and his understanding of this particular team's dynamics dictate how to proceed. No matter what, he will seek to connect with the team emotionally.

He could challenge the team's self-image: "Come on, I'm feeling pretty disappointed now, because I thought we were some of the most competitive people in the business. I never expected this team to be so willing to accept defeat."

He could appeal to team members' creativity: "Come on, I can't believe you don't have any clever insights on this one yet. I know this is the most creative team in the company. We are only one idea away from solving this!"

He could show his curiosity: "I am very curious right now, probably as curious as I have ever felt, because I'm wondering what a team with this much talent can do on such short notice and still pull off a miracle."

He could share his fear: "I have to tell you that I'm nervous about what it means if we can't figure this out. If we don't turn this around, they may push our product totally off the shelf." This is an authentic appeal from a place of fear, and the message is that an immediate solution is essential to survival in this market. Although fear is not a sustainable source of motivation, when it comes out of accurate reality testing, it can be the wake-up call we need to get going!

The leader's choice of the emotion to use is based on an intimate understanding of the team's emotional psyche. An appeal that yields excellent results with one team may fail with another. It depends on the team and the situation; no two are identical.

At first glance, this may seem like a clever ploy, manipulating words to push different buttons. It might be possible for an average leader to get away with trying that a time or two. But the team is smart. The team knows the difference between authenticity and manipulation. An authentic leader is transparent enough to naturally express his or her true feelings, and it is that very act that opens up the team's receptivity to the reservoir of emotional energy that is present in every situation. The leader's ability to reflect the team mood accurately and congruently can help the team mobilize all its problem-solving efforts.

The ESI leader helps the team channel its own emotional energy to close the gap between where they are and where they need to be. Depending on how the leader makes this request for accountability, it could create an element of guilt. Guilt is the feeling that arises out of the discrepancy between what we have committed to do and know we "should" do compared with our actual performance. It generates a "move away" response that can be very effective, especially when coupled with some real incentive to move toward the specific behaviors that will make the team more productive. If guilt is used too often and is not paired with a positive alternative or it degrades into shaming and humiliation, the leader will rapidly lose credibility and influence.

Influence is the power that a group of individuals cedes to a leader in order to receive the benefit of his or her leadership. It is far more effective than the power of position or wealth or fierceness or physical strength that less emotionally intelligent leaders use. Influence can never be demanded; it can only be earned, and just as certainly it can be lost. Influence is never lost by holding people accountable and asking them to do difficult things. In fact, when they succeed, that experience often significantly strengthens the leader's effectiveness. Influence is lost or earned in direct proportion to a leader's transparency and capability. Disrespect, double standards, emotional tyranny, dishonesty, and egotism are some of the emotionally unintelligent behaviors that quickly undermine one's effectiveness.

THE SEVEN SKILLS OF ESI LEADERSHIP

The following provides a summary of ways the leader can use each of the seven ESI skills to generate the four collaborative results—empathy, trust, loyalty, and better decisions—all of which evolve from applying the seven ESI skills.

POSITIVE MOOD

Successful ESI leadership is a result of building trust through respect. An emotionally and socially intelligent leader will blend all seven ESI skills in different degrees for different situations. An ESI leader doesn't need to use all the skills all the time. Perfection is not required! And all seven may not be relevant in every situation. Many leaders start their personal trek to ESI leadership by using positive mood because it's one of the easiest skills to implement. It's also one of the most effective.

By setting the pace with a genuinely optimistic outlook, a smile, good eye contact, energetic tonality, and purposeful gestures, the leader is demonstrating and teaching the team how to behave. These small acts set behavioral expectations right from the start. In spite of our independence, human beings have a strong inclination to follow the example of those around us who behave like leaders—congruent, clear-spoken, authoritative. Recall that the nonverbal signals are even more potent than the verbal communication, so you must do your best to use them with conscious skillfulness.

Positive mood enables the leader to reflect both the strengths and weaknesses of the team's members accurately and respectfully and to help them *want* to access the resourcefulness and resilience they need. In *Managing the Equity Factor*, Huseman and Hatfield report that nearly 85 percent of participants in their survey "said that they could work harder on the job. More than half claimed they could *double* their effectiveness 'if they wanted to'" (1989, p. 4).

If you as a leader have something valuable to contribute, it is the ability to help people "want to" do more. And the most powerful way to help people "want to" is to demonstrate your own "want to" in everything you do. As we noted earlier, using positive mood effectively also supports the skill of motivation. That's how it is in team life—these skills all work together.

EMOTIONAL AWARENESS

In the emotionally intelligent team leader, emotional awareness is as fundamental as it is broad. As a leader, you identify and understand your own emotions. You know how they influence your relationships and your own performance. You know your own strengths and stretches. You've got self-confidence. You are comfortable with yourself without being arrogant or self-important.

You can also read the internal states of your team members and interpret the state of the team as a whole. Your capacity for emotional awareness is intertwined with your empathy. You can figure out someone's emotional pulse by synthesizing the verbal and nonverbal cues.

In a kingdom far, far away, at the edge of a mighty forest, you come upon a person splitting wood at a ferocious pace. The split wood is stacked neatly in a short column, but behind the woodcutter is a large pile of logs yet to be split. You greet the woodcutter and inquire what's up with the intense log-splitting. The woodcutter could offer a few different reasons for the activity. Being quite practical, this individual might answer, "Winter is coming sooner than we thought, and I'll need this fuel to keep my family warm."

It's also possible that the woodcutter is having a bad day. The woodcutter might tersely reply, "I have just been misled by someone I trusted, and I'm so angry, I'll split his skull if I don't split this wood!" (An emotionally intelligent choice of great wisdom, by the way.)

The woodcutter might say, "It's such a beautiful day, and I so enjoy the exercise I get splitting wood, that I am having a bit of a contest with myself to see how much I can split."

Which of these motivations is likely to produce the most split wood? An emotionally intelligent leader knows that as strong a motivator as anger is, it will burn itself out, especially when it's channeled into a physically demanding activity like chopping wood. If the woodcutter is chopping to get exercise, that activity will likely produce only a modest amount of wood as well. If the woodcutter is worried about how much fuel will be available to heat the family's home in the winter, that concern causes him to set the pace in a completely different way. In this case, the woodcutter truly needs to get the whole pile split and then perhaps go cut more logs to make another pile. Here the woodcutter is in it for the long haul and has the most to lose or gain from the results.

The ability to understand why people are working and how much satisfaction they are getting from their work is the skill of an emotionally intelligent leader. That leader will be able to discern and deliver the balance of emotional and cognitive rewards that suit each team member and also produce the best results on behalf of the team.

TEAM IDENTITY

The ESI team leader will do everything possible to make belonging to the team a valuable reward in itself. Individuals naturally need a sense of belonging. We are social creatures. Recall that belonging needs are third in Maslow's hierarchy, after security and biological survival needs have been met. When a team's work is challenging enough, exciting enough, and safe enough for its members to contribute to it at full tilt without having to do a lot of posturing and defending, it makes going to work almost like coming home.

Team identity is enhanced by the way the team is managed and led. It is incumbent on the leader to facilitate open communication within the team. This doesn't happen by accident. Begging people to be honest doesn't do it either. Creating a sense of psychological security by making it safe to tell the truth without negative repercussions and building the expectation that truth will be told goes a long way toward strengthening the trust that individual team members need in order to learn not only how to respond to each other effectively but also how to accurately anticipate what the needed response might be. This dynamic also fosters a spirit of generous support and praise among the team, and that positive feedback enhances performance and team identity.

A cartoon we have seen on too many office walls has a caption that reads, "The beatings will continue until morale improves!" Though surely intended by the original author as a clever irony, all too often employees have posted it to protest the quality of working conditions. No one wants to be on such a team, and rightly so; the loss of synergy that those people could realize in better circumstances is immeasurable.

To be honest, teamwork is not a fairy tale. Everything doesn't turn out "happily every after" every time. Mistakes and losses must be accounted for and recovered from, and if you have a high-performing team, it should be making mistakes. Mistakes should be acknowledged and used as a tool for learning. Mistakes, shortcomings, partial fixes, and proposals that are off the mark or off budget can all inspire further innovation through constructive feedback. The key is that the feedback must be behaviorally based. One of the items on our team ESI assessment, the TESI, is "We constructively critique each other's work, not the person." Emotionally and socially intelligent team leaders cook up their own recipes for success from the seven basic ESI skills and use them as the foundation for strengthening communication and team identity.

MOTIVATION

Mahatma Gandhi, Harriet Tubman, Vince Lombardi, Joan of Arc, César Chávez, Winston Churchill, Oprah Winfrey—these powerful people share numerous commonalities, although nothing about them is common. They each have been able to motivate groups of people to move beyond obstacles and limitations and achieve unprecedented success. To instill in people the desire, the drive, the determination to persevere and to succeed is a skill with value beyond measure. Often the best way to understand the significance of instilling motivation is to imagine "what would never have happened" had it not been for the motivation to succeed against all odds. Motivation drives personal satisfaction and organizational outcomes.

You can succeed at motivating your team only if you care. All the carrots and sticks in the world are not nearly as effective as genuine human caring. When you demonstrate true concern for your team members, you not only motivate them but also learn who they are, what they care about, and how much they can contribute if you support them. Your efforts to help solve the team's challenges can simultaneously engage them around goals that have personal meaning, and productivity can skyrocket.

STRESS TOLERANCE

Dealing with the causes of stress and the strategies for reducing it is so central to the biological health of all team members that their leader needs to both model stress tolerance and teach stress reduction tactics regularly. One way to do this is to measure the stress level with a simple survey. Hand out a small card or piece of paper with five boxes on it. Ask the team members to check the box indicating the degree of stress they are experiencing. The boxes might be labeled as follows:

1. Bring It On—my responsibilities are well enough under control that I can help out if someone else on the team is crashing.
2. Just Enough Stress—the level is optimal; less stress would probably indicate that we are insufficiently engaged with the team goals.
3. More Than Enough—things are getting kind of edgy.
4. Way More Than Enough—work isn't fun anymore, and things will be falling off my plate if any more is expected of me.
5. Crashing—the stress level is over the top; the team's goals and my health are both suffering.

If *any* team member marks the 5 box, you have a problem. The leader needs to explore this feedback with tact, directness, and good reality testing so that the situation can be addressed and rectified. Perhaps no one could ever do this much work, or perhaps it is the wrong individual for this job.

The team and its members thrive when the level of stress is a 2 or 3 on that 5-point scale. The survey should be anonymous so that it's safe to tell the truth. The pressure to avoid looking incompetent or seeming like a burden to the team can be significant. Don't underestimate how pride can skew the scale.

If there is a highly competitive attitude among team members, such a survey may be of no use whatsoever because the incentive is to look good rather than to tell the truth. In that case, simply helping team members learn how to make each other feel valued will go further in reducing the stress level than probably anything else. When they feel safer in their working environment, they won't feel the obsessive need to achieve that leads to mistakes and more stress. Competition within such a team has to be carefully monitored, even discouraged to some extent, until a high level of trust is accomplished. The exception to this is a sales team within an organizational culture that is designed to reward individual top-performing contributors.

COMMUNICATION

As the leader, it's up to you to expand your communication repertoire so that you can be effective with the team. If you're leading an emotionally intelligent team, this should be reasonably fun. Your messages should be direct, specific, and designed to skillfully negotiate the filters and biases that your team members may have. Keep in mind the tremendous effect that nonverbal communication has on the recipient.

Most important, the ESI team leader will communicate from a place of self-regard that reflects authenticity, openness, and a deep trust in the communication process. Allow for silence. It gives time for people to process and reflect. It models thoughtful responses to difficult and complex issues. Having the right response on the tip of the tongue is not always the most effective way to communicate. Allowing time for reflection facilitates the deeper insight on which innovation relies.

CONFLICT RESOLUTION

Resolving conflict skillfully is advanced ESI work. It takes the most effort. It's also among the most important skills a leader has. Healthy conflict is a positive force on the team. It instills creativity, promotes problem solving, and leads to innovation. However, the inherent good found in conflict can be accessed only if the team is imbued with values that respect and support diversity on all levels. Conflict can be a gold mine if you're skilled at identifying the nuggets and refining them. As a leader, you must welcome conflict and work with all the intelligence of the team if it is going to influence the problem-solving process in the most beneficial way. Team members do not avoid expressing their thoughts, feelings, and opinions when conflict is treated as a challenge to be investigated rather than a contest to be won. And avoiding conflict entirely seriously diminishes the value that your team can produce.

By teaching team members to acknowledge that multiple realities can coexist and to use language patterns that challenge others' point of view respectfully, the leader helps team members become more comfortable with differing perspectives. A glass can accurately be described as half full or half empty or simply too large or too small a glass—it's all in your point of view.

Encourage conversation about topics from all vantage points. Discuss optical illusions and abstract art to demonstrate there are lots of different ways to see "reality." Role-play different perspectives so that people learn to walk a mile in someone else's shoes. Your team members will begin transforming into people who are less attached to being right and more invested in a collaborative process of developing solutions that have considered and incorporated multiple points of view.

One of the ways for a leader to empower and liberate the capacities of the team is to help each person develop a unique spirit to demonstrate competency and self-regard. Performing competently and successfully in your work and being respected for it are at the heart of the fourth level of Maslow's hierarchy, your esteem needs. For some people, it's a new idea that you can increase your self-regard without it being at the expense of another. Team life is not a zero-sum game. It's a win-win opportunity. It takes a little practice for some people to learn how to acknowledge and praise the work of others without feeling personally diminished, but little else will go as far to build trust and identity among the members of your team.

Conclusion

It's a smart move to take personal responsibility for developing your leadership capacities, whether you are formally recognized as the team leader or not. In some aspect of your life, you *are* the official leader—whether it's as a parent, a coach, a tribal elder, or a seasoned volunteer. And in any case, you are the boss of your own life, which is an important opportunity to lead!

You'd be surprised at how often the emotionally intelligent team leader is someone other than the person who has the official title. Servant-leadership plays an increasingly important role in the larger workplace of fierce global competition, and an individual with a high level of social responsibility can effect sustainable changes for the greater social good. There is no lack of work to be done and no lack of individuals who will show up to do it when emotionally and socially intelligent leaders confidently apply the seven ESI skills.

Chapter Twelve

VALUES AND ETHICS

Things which matter most must never be at the mercy
of things which matter least.
Johann Wolfgang von Goethe

Vanessa jubilantly burst into Paul's office.

"Paul, you've got to look at this. I think I've finally nailed down the new glass-making process for the insulation. Take a look; I want to make sure I didn't overlook anything." She nearly threw the documents on his desk in her excitement.

Paul was intrigued. "I'll take a look and get back to you in a day or two," he replied. "I'm swamped with production forecasts at the moment."

The next morning dawned bright with promise. Vanessa was still buzzing when she arrived at the team meeting. Jackie, their manager, started right on time. "I got some great news from Paul," she began. "He's made phenomenal strides in developing a new process for making glass for our insulation. It moves us much closer to owning that market!"

Paul accepted the praise with enthusiasm, studiously avoiding looking at Vanessa. Vanessa's mouth opened, but nothing came out as she glared at Paul. Rage boiled within her. She could not believe what had just happened.

This is a team in trouble. At least one member is significantly compromising his ethical behavior, and another is going to have to dig deep to find her best conflict resolution skills so that she doesn't destroy her own reputation when she blows the whistle on Paul.

THE FOUNDATION OF WORKPLACE VALUES

When teams face difficult choices about how to get their work done, their values can serve as road signs to help them make the critical decisions about where they want to go and the best route to get there. Our values condense thousands of years of our ancestors' decision-making experience and give us huge advantage toward achieving the goals that build a team's success.

For instance, the idea that "honesty is the best policy" probably has analogues reaching back into ancient Roman, Greek, and Chinese societies. Anytime a society has reached a high level of integration and produced great achievements in commerce, literature, art, and government, teams of individuals at some level have agreed to tell the truth—at least to each other. Certainly, significant deception was employed to confuse one's enemies and provoke competition among one's rivals for power and glory in these societies, but the people who achieved the greatest accomplishments and got the most real work done were those who were communicating the most clearly and openly with each other about their intentions, plans, actions, and the results of their efforts.

Vanessa and Paul appear to be on different sides of the great divide in the ongoing values discussion that has engaged our species since its earliest days: which of the two antagonistic survival strategies shall we employ—cooperation or competition?

We all have at least rudimentary skills in both of these strategies, but all of us have been deeply exposed to the world of competition and know all too well how to defend and attack and deceive. That is because competition is a strategy that is easy to understand and simple to master. You merely have to decide who are your "friends" and who are your "enemies" and then tell your "enemies" half-truths and lies and use all of your intelligence and power to satisfy your needs at their expense.

To succeed, you will need the allegiance and cooperation of your "friends," so tell them 90 percent of the truth about your intentions (even 95 percent if you really trust them!). And leverage all of your combined resources to "win," meaning to defeat your "enemies."

This is what we imagine must have been the real world story of team values since our ancestors lived in caves and were employed as hunter-gatherers. But we may have missed something.

Chris Argyris's (1994) work on the ladder of inference has shown how we tend to perceive what we expect because our brain is able to function with a feature called selective memory. Recent memories are flagged with a marker for importance that often gives them disproportionate weight in our assessment of reality. Neuroscientists like Candace Pert and metaphysicians as far back as Mary Baker Eddy (if not farther) have pointed out that we are as likely to see what we believe as we are to believe what we see.

Seeing the world as a seething hotbed of competition makes perfect sense in a globalizing planetary economy. Jobs from the developed world are outsourced to laborers in the developing world, who are paid a tiny fraction of the wages of the people who created or implemented the technological and business processes in the first place. But the science that gave rise to a vast amount of that technology—from the microwaves in our kitchens to the lasers in our CD players—emerged from our discovery that the universe that is not antagonistic but extraordinarily holistic, integrated, and complementary.

Understanding quantum physics at the most detailed theoretical level isn't rocket science—it's much more difficult! But it is not outlandish to seek to reconcile the best practices of teamwork with our best science. Let's start by considering some of the values that we know from experience are necessary for high-performing teams.

HONESTY

Honesty is at the center of all effective teamwork and sustainable productivity. It means that we do what we say we will do to the very best of our ability and that if we cannot live up to our commitments, we will inform the people who are depending on us at the earliest possible moment. It means we give them all the information they legitimately need and expect and no misleading information.

What gives honesty such high priority as a value? Human beings work to meet the needs that will keep them alive and satisfy the desires that give their lives meaning. When we work together, we can accomplish vastly more than we could ever dream of accomplishing alone. When we're working together in that magical state our friends at Team Coaching International call "high productivity–high positivity," our experience of performing effectively is highly motivating and a joy in itself.

But that can't happen if we can't trust each other. Creativity can only grow in a climate of openness. If we have to be on guard, holding the thought in the back of our mind that someone may try to take credit for our work, our subconscious will act out of self-preservation and make sure our best work never gets out.

RESPECT

Respect is every bit as important as honesty, and in fact it is often our respect for our teammates that ensures that we will be honest with them. Respect is born in an interesting place: it comes from our sensitivity.

The images we see, the sounds we hear, the touch of the external world on our skin, our sense of smell and taste—all of these things enter our awareness through our body in vulnerable places. When that vulnerability has been respected by others, we naturally appreciate it and respect it in them. When that vulnerability has been treated harshly or disrespectfully, we are likely to lose some of our own sensitivity and thus lose some of our ability to appreciate it and respond to it in others.

It is possible we will not even know this has happened until perhaps we receive feedback from a 360-degree assessment of our emotional effectiveness. Then, if we are brave enough to take the risks and disciplined enough to sustain the effort, we can successfully resensitize ourselves to the needs and desires of the people around us. As our respect for them increases, our empathy increases. Or if we work at it from the other direction, as we learn how to be more open, sensitive, and empathic, respect for our teammates increases. In either case, trust between us grows.

Respect is the care that we take of each other, the courage to be open and sensitive to each other's needs, the honesty to tell the truth about what we think and feel, and the patience to maintain our resourcefulness when someone falls short or makes a mistake.

Fair Compensation

Fair compensation is actually an extension of both respect and honesty, but it is the value that often carries more weight than all the others, and there have been many reports about the huge discrepancies between what people at the top of an organization are paid compared to those at the entry level. We'll explore that in more depth, but first, we would like to provide some context with the following story.

For many years, James had the privilege of interviewing guests on a local cable television show called *Spiritual Spectrum*. It was the brainchild of producer Dave Edwards, who had decided it would be interesting to regularly get a group of people together from a variety of different religious backgrounds and have them discuss what they *agreed* on. The guests were intelligent, funny, passionate, and mature enough not to take themselves too seriously, so it wasn't that much of a challenge to moderate the show. The host's biggest challenge usually was to get enough powder on his head to dull the reflectivity, and so it went for two years.

Then James decided he wanted to produce a show himself on an ecological topic that had deeply engaged his interest and concern. Although the crew members were already volunteering their time, they all agreed to fill in their regular positions for yet another show if he was willing to *organize* it. (That's a simplistic description of what the producer does.)

Suddenly James, who had always seen himself as a rugged individualist who highly valued self-sufficiency, discovered how profoundly dependent he and the show were on teamwork! Even before James arrived, the lighting engineer had already spent sixty to ninety minutes getting all the lights positioned correctly for the small set, where four to six people simply sat around a coffee table. The producer had driven to the media supply house and purchased the professional-grade 1¼-inch videotape, and he or the director had done all the character generation to get the correctly spelled name of each guest to appear on-screen when they were speaking for the first time, not to mention all the titles and the credits. The director had set up the video recorder and all the microphones and had adjusted the volume level for the guests, positioned and white-balanced each of the three cameras and tested his headset communications with each camera operator, confirmed that the microphones and instruments for the live music introduction were working, and then directed the show. The producer had rounded up the live music and all the guests, given them maps with instructions to the studio, obtained their signed releases, purchased the live flowers, set the stage, and then struck it when the show was over. So much for self-sufficiency!

There are no stars or superstars whose impressive show does not depend on teams of talented and hardworking people to make a seemingly effortless performance happen. It could be as small as the team that cleans and fills your teeth or the vast organization that brings you the Olympic Games.

Yet in 2005, the ratio of executive compensation to employee pay in the United States was 411 to 1. That's up considerably from 1990, when the ratio was 100 to 1, but down a little since 2000, when the sixteen-year average topped out at 525 to 1. That means if you were making a little more than the federal minimum wage in 2005, say, $6 an hour, the CEO was making more than $2,466 per hour.

To work well together, team members must be secure in the knowledge that at the end of the day their efforts will more than meet their families' survival needs. Effective team members are motivated to achieve both personal and organizational values. From an organizational perspective, they will certainly do a better job when they feel that financial and quality-of-life incentives are available to reward innovation and commitment.

Employees' personal needs include expecting that their good work will be acknowledged by their leaders in front of their coworkers every so often and that work above and beyond the call of duty might be recognized with a ceremony or even an award. Anticipating being rewarded with some time off every year and being able to afford a nice vacation in a special place every couple of years, along with sufficient health care and enough money for retirement, makes commitment to the job much easier. And when their work feels meaningful because they know they helped others live more comfortable and fulfilling lives, that completes the type of compensation package most people whose personal and social priorities are in balance want, will work for, and will flourish under. This is the foundation for motivating your team.

EFFICIENT USE OF RESOURCES

Using resources and time efficiently is a value that most people in organizations understand because both are in limited supply. Some people recognize this more clearly than others and train themselves to notice where they can create and take advantage of economies of scale.

Teams can't thrive without knowing and noticing those who care enough to work efficiently. Efficiency is not a science, it's an art, but it doesn't happen by accident; it reflects how we use the executive centers of the prefrontal cortex to envision and plan our work or to cut unnecessary steps out of the simple routines that make up daily life. In any case, it is an acquired skill that demands care, attention, practice, and trial and error, even if it's just to make the right amount of coffee for the team so that no one goes without at the beginning of a long day and that you don't end up throwing a full pot away.

Efficiency requires coordination between team members, regular practice, as well as individual commitment. When it is inspired by genuine respect and appreciation for the planet and her vast diversity of resources, our efficiency honors the time and efforts of our organization, our teammates, and ourselves. The old adage of "waste not, want not" is an accurate expression of the universe's primeval strategy for maintaining natural balance.

Growing up on both sides of the Continental Divide in Colorado during the 1950s and 1960s, neither of us ever saw bison in the wild. Their value as livestock was yet to be discovered, so they, like the Native Americans who had lived in spiritual balance with them, were few and far between. But there was a saying that the immigrant Americans still told sometimes while "camping" where the Cheyenne, Arapaho, Kiowa, and Ute had lived not so very long ago. It was an echo of the contrasting values between two civilizations that characterized the indigenous voice like this: "White man build big fire, stand way back. Indian build little fire, sit up close." How wisely does your team use its resources? Does it sit up close or stand way back from embracing the discipline necessary to implement the critical value of sustainability?

Values are rules of thumb that we honor and obey because they reflect the nature of the universe and our teams' reality. They are both what is practical and what works!

What you and your team expect to show up in the world will have a significant effect on the challenges and solutions you experience and hence the values you choose to guide your behavior. If you expect conflict and turf battles because there is a limited amount of compensation and recognition and you are determined to get yours, you'd better watch your back. If you expect to be treated respectfully and handle any rudeness you experience as a weird fluke that is highly unusual on your team, you will find both trust and productivity growing.

The advanced quantum models of the universe reveal reality to be an omnipresent field of energy and information that is ordered at the deepest level by a singularity that connects and unifies and runs through all the objects and events that appear to be separate from our human point of view. Quantum theorists tell us it is as if there is really only one super being living a single life that is everything going on everywhere, manifesting its presence through every chess game, flea, comet, and concerto that has ever been or ever will be. If that is so, perhaps we neglect to value our deep relatedness with all the members of Team Earth at our own peril.

We have said that it is easier to perceive life as a contest, that competition is a simple strategy to learn and understand, but what that ignores is the fact that we have to disregard this fundamental wholeness in order to compete with each other in our winner-take-all fashion. Constructive competition in which a team wins a bonus for its creativity or persistent diligence is a great thing and provides the level of challenge and incentive that human beings need to keep their edge and stay innovative. Yet taken too far, competition destroys team spirit.

When the stakes in the game get ratcheted up to the place where Paul is trying to steal credit for Vanessa's creativity, we can only hope she has read this book (especially the chapter on conflict resolution) and has the emotional and social intelligence necessary to confront him and engage their manager with the appropriate level of assertiveness, empathy, and self-regard. Yes, Vanessa, even when dealing with those who seem like jerks, there is still great value in using empathy!

CHAPTER THIRTEEN

RESULTS

The greatest discovery of my generation is that human beings can alter their lives by altering their attitudes of mind.
WILLIAM JAMES

Investing in your team's ESI skills will significantly increase the quality of your team's results. It is the proven path to sustainable productivity. Highly developed ESI skills provide the critical foundation for success. The consulting firm of Hay/McBer conducted a research study at a large beverage company that showed that division heads who had strong ESI skills outperformed targets by 15 to 20 percent and those who lacked those competencies underperformed by about 20 percent. ESI is about results (McClelland, 1999). In August 2002, a large, multifacility hospital system turned to us to help conduct team-building retreats for its corporate marketing and public relations department. The organization had just gone through a period of transition after merging with another company, hiring some new managers, and opening a new hospital. Just building and opening a new hospital was no small thing.

The original goal of the retreat was to find ways for people in the department to work together more productively and fit into the new culture the organization sought to foster. However, when we arrived on-site, we found extreme distress among the team, and that needed immediate attention before a retreat would do any good. The turmoil was intense. Without resolution, there could be no positive results. Their leader had divided the staff into two camps—those he favored and those he didn't. Even the favored staff was on edge. Displeasing the boss with even one small thing could cause a favored team member to become persona non grata. Staff members who weren't favored were treated brutally. One team member came in to find a report she had given the manager taped to her office door. It was heavily marked up with a red pen and a big note to get the report cleaned up NOW! It was utterly dispiriting. This formerly vibrant team felt assaulted and berated.

Fortunately, the senior vice president recognized that there was a big problem. She jumped in and gave it her full attention. Dealing with this crisis required several immediate and major steps concurrently. We responded rapidly, doing intense work with the staff immediately to boost their ESI skills so that they could face challenges with a sense of support and encouragement. The most essential competencies began with stress management, communication, and conflict resolution. It wasn't easy, but it was indispensable. Over the course of a few months, the dynamics changed. The organization's executives began immediate action to resolve the situation. They sought a new manager for the department. The actions of the senior team invigorated the staff. This responsiveness reinforced the staff's newfound behaviors and enhanced their resilience.

The team also needed to understand what resources it had among the staff. A strategic assessment of each team member was developed to understand personality preferences, strengths and weaknesses, and the ESI skills the person could bring to the team. Sharing the results with the team members provided each team member with significant information. Information is empowering, and the team felt it! The members developed a new awareness of their capabilities and began to enhance their capacity. Their stress declined, which helped them relax, and that gave them more energy and better thinking.

In the months to come, even as the team worked amid a fair amount of uncertainty, the organization's executives saw a greater sense of loyalty emerge. As evidence of this, not one member of the department's staff left the organization during this time of challenge and transition. Now, several years later, the team members are still close. Only a few have left—one to join a family business, one to work in another part of the organization, and one to run a consulting business from home while raising her children. Not surprisingly, this team is her best client, and her colleagues love to see her kids growing up. The team is resilient, gets its work out promptly, and has improved channels of communication throughout the hospital system, more efficiently spreading the marketing message.

INTEGRATING ESI BEHAVIORS FOR SUCCESS

What that health care organization was able to achieve is indicative of the potential for every team. The increasing body of emotional intelligence research shows that cultivating ESI behaviors yields success. Teamwork makes the world go round. While the idea of teamwork is as old as the human species, it's more relevant today than it has ever been. The emotional intelligence of the team dictates its success. Teams that create an emotionally intelligent environment that supports the seven ESI skills of team identity, motivation, emotional awareness, effective communication, stress tolerance, conflict resolution, and positive mood are nurturing four essential results for success: empathy, trust, loyalty, and better decision making. Ultimately, this package yields sustained productivity and teams of people who care about each other and like to work together.

Goethe captured the importance of developing a foundation such as we're talking about when he reportedly said: "I respect the [team] who knows distinctly what they wish. The greater part of all mischief in the world arises from the fact that people do not sufficiently understand their own aim. They have undertaken to build a tower, and spend no more labor on the foundation than would be necessary to erect a hut."

Invest in a strong foundation for your team, and you gain big results—trust, empathy, loyalty, and better decisions. And it doesn't stop there. These results lead to sustainable productivity and emotional and social well-being for the team and its members. That's the stuff of a healthy and vibrant organization. That spells wealth. And it creates an environment where you want to work.

Building Your Team's Collaborative Intelligence

The progressive benefits of developing a team's ESI are reflected in the model shown in Figure 13.1, which demonstrates the circles of influence surrounding a team's emotional and social intelligence. As that intelligence radiates inward to the inner circle, it integrates to become your team's collaborative intelligence. The outer circle is composed of the seven skills or behaviors that are the building

Figure 13.1.   From Emotional Intelligence to Collaborative Intelligence: A Team Model.

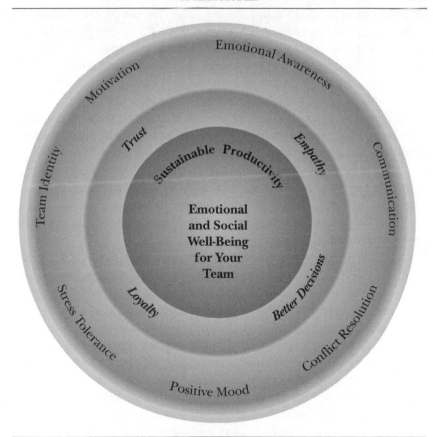

blocks of ESI for teams. The middle circle reflects the highly desired results teams and their organizations need most: empathy, trust, loyalty, and better decisions. Finally, the inner core leads us to the long-term benefits of sustainable productivity and emotional and social well-being for teams and their individual members. When this circle radiates its power, you have collaborative intelligence.

Take a look at the four results a team gains when it uses the seven skills effectively.

EMPATHY

Empathy is such a salient and valuable part of emotional and social intelligence that we have directed your attention to it throughout the book. Empathy is not about simply being nice to colleagues, nor is it about allowing emotions to rule the day. Just the opposite—it's about responding with compassion and understanding, thereby creating stronger bonds and reducing the risk that colliding emotions will cause spontaneous combustion or a team meltdown. It's a compelling outcome of using the seven ESI behaviors skillfully, and it does more for the enduring well-being and sustained productivity of the team than just about anything else. Because empathy is such a powerful result, it's bigger than any one skill. Hence empathy resides in the middle circle of influence linking skills to the results you, your team, and your organization need and value as essential to success.

Empathy shows up in team behavior when one team member listens attentively to another. It happens when you're able to listen openly and respectfully to one another's stories and get a real sense of the emotional engagement. It happens when you're willing to show compassion.

Recently, a colleague of ours, Lorenzo, went through one of the most gut-wrenching, agonizing experiences that a human can face. His son Martin was hospitalized with a life-threatening illness. Lorenzo's boss, Christopher, knew about it but never said a word to him. He didn't console Lorenzo, express his concern, or even offer him extra time off work. Lorenzo took the time anyway but felt hurt, betrayed, and angry beyond measure. Thankfully, Martin made a full recovery. Later Lorenzo confronted Christopher about his lack of caring. He found out that Christopher's silence was due to embarrassment and discomfort.

Christopher said, "I always consider family matters very personal, and I didn't want to intrude, so I just tried to stay out of your way." Lorenzo's anger diminished when he heard this, but it didn't dissipate completely. The explanation helped, but it wasn't enough. No surprise. The intensity and immensity of the event demanded that Christopher take notice. There are times when it is critical for a boss to speak up and acknowledge an employee's reality. The team would be stronger if the supervisor had developed the emotional awareness and communication skills necessary for expressing empathy. His example would have inspired the team to rally and support their colleague, instead of leaving Lorenzo feeling abandoned.

Strong empathy is a powerful emotion that can sustain team members, make them more resilient, and improve team spirit and collaboration. Empathy seems a soft word, but it should command the utmost respect because its power to sustain the team and generate productivity is unparalleled.

TRUST

Trust is the glue that holds teams together. A team's emotional and social intelligence is inextricably linked to the behavior that builds relationships. Creating strong bonds gives teams the emotional capital to persevere under duress and to face tough challenges that require flexible and creative problem solving. A trusting environment promotes risk taking, outside-the-box thinking, and innovation. Trust is developed as a consequence of team attitude, acting with integrity, and a willingness to be vulnerable.

Trust is what makes teams powerful. In 1982, seven people in the Chicago area died from ingesting cyanide-laced Tylenol capsules. Sales instantly stopped, with good reason: the public had no trust in the product. People wondered whether the manufacturer, Johnson & Johnson, could ever recover from the debacle. However, J&J rallied under the impressive leadership of its chairman, James E. Burke. The company made consumer safety its top priority, regardless of all else. It recalled every bottle of Tylenol from every store shelf in the country and urged consumers not to take any Tylenol until it could be determined how the tampering happened. J&J reached out to establish communication with the FBI and the Chicago police and offered a $100,000 reward for information leading to the arrest of the culprit. The company was compassionate and candid throughout the ordeal. Within five months of the tragedy, Johnson & Johnson had come up with the first tamperproof drug package in the country and recaptured about 70 percent of its market share.

Johnson & Johnson turned to the company's credo, written by company founder Robert Wood Johnson in the mid-1940s. Johnson believed that the company had social responsibilities, not just bottom-line responsibilities. He believed that it was responsible to the public and medical professionals who used its products, to its employees, to the communities where its employees lived, and to its stockholders. Johnson was a passionate believer that honoring all these responsibilities would result in long-term success.

That credo served as the company's moral compass. With strong leadership and high internal trust and integrity, the company was able to rebound and restore the public's confidence. It was a remarkable demonstration of the powerful results a company can achieve when it uses ESI skills. When teams seek to increase their influence by strengthening or rebuilding trust, they should focus on three attributes:

1. *Attitude* is demonstrated by the members' faith in the value of the team. Their belief that the team and its mandate are worthy of their identification and personal investment is essential and becomes manifest through body posture, open direct communication, and maintaining internal and external respect for the team's reputation.
2. *Integrity* is defined as the quality of possessing and steadfastly adhering to high moral principles or professional standards. It also reflects completeness and wholeness. Team members must be able to rely on one another to act with honesty and integrity or they will not be able to trust one another or the team process. This is a black-and-white criterion. However, it can be applied to some and not others when teams have selective trust around the table. They can know based on real experience that some members of their team can be trusted and some cannot. Human beings choose the level of competence they will bestow on each person individually.

This half-a-loaf is much better than nothing. If that's what you have, use it as best as possible and seek to grow to full trust.

3. *Vulnerability* reflects the ability to tell the truth and take risks with one another.

Robert Hurley, professor of management at Fordham University, wrote an article titled "The Decision to Trust" (2006). He has created a ten-point functional list to evaluate a team's level of trust. The first three components are based on the individual's personality—risk tolerance, level of adjustment, and how much power the person holds. The remaining seven are environmental conditions: security, communication, predictability and integrity, benevolent concern, number of similarities, capability, and alignment of interests. Notice which of these result directly from using the seven ESI skills.

Trust works best when it's modeled by the team leader. Peter Drucker, the management guru, is well known for pointing out that effective leaders emphasize the team, and it shows up in their language. Those leaders use the words "we" or "our team" much more often than "I." They think in terms of "we" and "team," not "me." Effective leaders are quick to accept personal responsibility for problems, but they share credit with the whole team. Consistently using this behavior builds trust. When the leader's behaviors are trustworthy, it becomes contagious. Team members are much more likely to trust one another when they have a compelling example to follow.

LOYALTY

The expectations of both organizations and employees about how long the employee relationship will continue have changed radically in the last few decades. Mobility is the ruling dynamic. Yet loyalty, redefined to meet today's environment, is more important than ever. The challenges imposed by global competition, new technologies, the rapid pace of change, and an aging workforce make loyalty a valuable competitive advantage. Millions of older employees are starting to exit the workforce, creating a talent shortage and a knowledge gap that will have a huge impact on companies and is triggering a major focus on succession planning. Loyalty counters turnover, supports the best succession plan, and saves money.

Loyalty is the result of applying the seven ESI behaviors and is an essential attribute of a strong team. Loyalty creates an environment that supports creativity, tenacity, synergy, and commitment.

BETTER DECISIONS

The defining criterion for a successful team is that it is able to make good decisions that accomplish its goals. This is so whether it's the music team for your church or the executive team for a *Fortune* 100 company. Good, strong, and sustainable decisions are facilitated by the seven ESI skills—every one of them is relevant, and the more they are applied by the team to its day-to-day functioning, the stronger and more lasting the decisions it makes will be.

When people feel positive and connected, they work better, and their mental acuity goes up. High ESI actually improves the team's ability to use its cognitive skills. Organizations develop high-performing teams by knowing how to value the old saying "Two heads are better than one." Research repeatedly shows that emotionally and socially intelligent teams make better decisions than individuals do. They apply ESI skills to build a level of synergy that completely surpasses teams with low ESI skills.

CELEBRATING SUSTAINABLE SUCCESS

It matters if you just don't give up.
STEPHEN HAWKING

Our team model pictures the incremental skills and benefits a team gains as it develops the seven core skills of ESI and then gains the four results of trust, empathy, loyalty, and better decisions. As these skills unfold, a team and its organization reach the most desired results of sustainable productivity and emotional and social well-being. We hope you feel inspired to go for the gold: reach for these superior benefits! They are obtainable by developing and using the skills we have been discussing throughout the book. Both of these golden results make a big difference.

SUSTAINABLE PRODUCTIVITY

Whole Foods Market is the world's leading retailer of natural and organic foods. It has close to two hundred stores in North America and the United Kingdom. It has been ranked among *Fortune* magazine's "Top 100 Companies to Work For" since the inception of the list. It is one of only eighteen companies to occupy a coveted spot on the list every year since it was launched in 1998. Those are impressive results!

What's more impressive is that in 2000, it was ranked seventy-second on the list. In 2007, it was ranked fifth. The company's motto is "Whole Foods, Whole People, Whole Planet." The company's primary focus is on customer satisfaction, team member excellence and happiness, return on capital investment, improvement in the state of the environment, and interdependence. Its leaders believe that better communication equals better understanding and more trust. Their commitment to high emotional and social intelligence is fundamental to their sustained productivity and the well-being of their team members.

John Mackey, Whole Foods CEO, reduced his salary to $1 a year, effective January 1, 2007, and is forgoing personal compensation from future stock options and funneling those monies to the company's two nonprofit foundations, the Whole Planet Foundation and the Animal Compassion Foundation. On November 2, 2006, he announced to his staff:

> The tremendous success of Whole Foods Market has provided me with far more money than I ever dreamed I'd have and far more than is necessary for either my financial security or personal happiness. I continue to work for Whole Foods not because of the money I can make but because of the pleasure I get from leading such a great company, and the ongoing passion I have to help make the world a better place, which Whole Foods is continuing to do. I am now 53 years old and I have reached a place in my life where I no longer want to work for money, but simply for the joy of the work itself and to better answer the call to service that I feel so clearly in my own heart.

Mackey's example is inspirational, but you don't have to forgo a paycheck to demonstrate high ESI! You also don't need to be perfect in the way you engage your emotional and social intelligence. No one individual is, and neither is any team. However, it is only through developing your team's ESI competencies that you will be able to deliver sustainable productivity. If you keep going for it, paying attention, having specific and focused positive intentions as you listen, speak, and act in coordination with one another, your team will develop the highest expression of these skills: collaborative intelligence. This is what is required to demonstrate the epitome of success: sustainable productivity and emotional and social well-being for all the members of your team.

The success that Whole Foods Markets has developed is a lofty example of what's possible for every team and organization that commits itself to fostering emotional and social intelligence. John Mackey and the highly valued teams at Whole Foods illustrate the truth that the search for money is really a search for meaning. Using the ESI skills effectively on your team to create that meaning and value is the prescription for sustainable productivity; it's the path to the inner circle, which radiates collaborative intelligence through using the seven skills and the power that results.

EMOTIONAL AND SOCIAL WELL-BEING FOR YOUR TEAM

> *Live for your days on, not your days off!*
> MARCIA HUGHES

We experience emotional well-being as a sense of balance and general harmony. Social well-being is reflected in the network of strong and trusting relationships that support our personal and professional lives. We know we're giving our gifts to the world; we feel productive and take time to enjoy life. We love others and receive their love in return. This is achievable for teams and their members when they intentionally apply all seven ESI skills. It's the result of persistence and taking the risks to be open and direct in all your communications. It's paying attention to how you live your life, individually and collectively as a team. Challenges will still arise, without a doubt. The difference is that a sense of internal well-being will be available to call on for support even when your project is late, your budget is cut, or your team doesn't get all the honors you believe you deserve.

Emotional and social well-being requires that your team has in place strategies for stress management to provide every member a shared cushion of resilience. It manifests when team members have each found the perfect pitch in their interactions and resonate in a powerful and harmonious chord. This awesome feeling becomes a sustainable part of team life when everyone shares the intention to apply the seven ESI skills and treats each day as a new opportunity built on a history of increased openness and commitment to results. This kind of optimism is the sustainable fuel of great teamwork! Embrace it. Enjoy it. Live it!

CONCLUSION

That only which we have within, can we see
without. If we meet no Gods, it is because we harbor
none. If there is a grandeur in you, you will find
grandeur in porters and sweeps.
RALPH WALDO EMERSON

Georgia O'Keeffe, the southwestern artist who is honored with a museum dedicated to her work in Santa Fe, New Mexico, is known for her brilliant, colorful paintings of simple objects from the desert. She once gave some advice that teams can benefit from if they take it to heart. O'Keeffe is oft quoted as admonishing that "nothing is less real than realism. Details are confusing. It is only by selection, by elimination, by emphasis that we get at the real meaning of things." After all this edification about the seven skills that build your team's emotional and social intelligence—dissecting them, analyzing them, applying them, synthesizing them, and finally getting results from them—it's possible to lose sight of the forest for all the many trees. Integrating the seven skills will yield highly prized results: trust, empathy, loyalty, and better decisions. Those four results lead to your team ultimately experiencing sustainable productivity and the resonance of emotional and social well-being.

After exploring emotional and social intelligence from numerous angles and turning it inside out, we recommend that you balance all that with O'Keeffe's advice. Don't get caught up trying to memorize every single detail and nuance. It doesn't work that way. Refrain from the mistaken belief that perfection can be achieved. Perfection is not the goal. It's all about the journey. You are much better served by sampling, selecting, blending, tweaking, and emphasizing what works best for your team's chemistry. Use your creative energies to claim your own process and results.

Emotional literacy is a key tool to use in making your decisions about what is meaningful for you and your team. Your literacy is simply your ability to read the social and emotional cues from one another, the group as a whole, and the social and political environment of your organization. Literacy improves with practice.

Finally, we can't resist emphasizing the value of taking reflective time with one another. Whether you are discussing what went well and why or what you'd like to improve or telling stories about your life and your role on the team, the reflective process allows you to examine your actions in order to be aware, stay responsive, and make good decisions. Teams who haven't lived an examined life don't have much to say, and their contributions are diminished. With the discipline of talking and listening through reflective awareness, you will tap into some of the best whole-brain collective wisdom your team has to offer. Enjoy the journey, and have patience!

We're in a cycle of continuous change and evolution. Thus we look to Richard Bach for inspiration during such whirlwind change. Bach wrote, "What the caterpillar calls the end of the world, the master calls a butterfly" (1977, p. 177). Spread your wings!

REFERENCES

Ambady, A., and Rosenthal, R. (1993). "Half a Minute: Predicting Teacher Evaluations from Thin Slices of Nonverbal Behavior and Physical Attractiveness." *Journal of Personality and Social Psychology*, 64: 431–441.

Argyris, C. (1994). *On Organizational Learning.* Oxford, UK: Blackwell.

Arnsten, A. (1998). "The Biology of Being Frazzled." *Science*, 280: 1711–1713.

Bach, R. (1977). *Illusions: The Adventures of a Reluctant Messiah.* New York: Dell.

Bar-On, R. (1997). *The Emotional Quotient Inventory (EQ-i): Technical Manual.* Toronto: Multi-Health Systems.

Bar-On, R. (2005). "The Bar-On Model of Emotional-Social Intelligence (ESI)." Available at http://www.eiconsortium.org/research/baron_model_of_emotional_social_intelligence.pdf.

Bar-On, R., Tranel, D., Denburg, N. L., and Bechara, A. (2003). "Exploring the Neurological Substrate of Emotional and Social Intelligence." *Brain*, 126: 1790–1800.

Barsade, S. (2002). "The Ripple Effect: Emotional Contagion and Its Influence on Group Behavior." *Administrative Science Quarterly*, 47: 644–675.

Beck, D. E. (n.d.). "Welcome to Spiral Dynamics." Available at http://www.spiraldynamics.net.

Beck, D. E., and Cowan, C. C. (1996). *Spiral Dynamics: Mastering Values, Leadership, and Change.* Malden, Mass.: Blackwell.

Boyatzis, R. E., and McKee, A. (2005). *Resonant Leadership: Renewing Yourself and Connecting with Others Through Mindfulness, Hope, and Compassion.* Boston: Harvard Business School Press.

Bryan, S. P. (2006). "Emotional Intelligence and Intrapersonal Conversations." Available at http://www.eiconsortium.org/research/emotional_intelligence_and_intrapersonal_communications.pdf.

Buckingham, M., and Clifton, D. O. (2001). *Now, Discover Your Strengths.* New York: Simon & Schuster.

Caruso, D. R., and Salovey, P. (2004). *The Emotionally Intelligent Manager.* San Francisco: Jossey-Bass.

Castaneda, C. (1998). *The Wheel of Time: The Shamans of Ancient Mexico, Their Thoughts About Life, Death, and the Universe.* Los Angeles: La Eidolona Press.

Cherniss, C. (2004). "Emotional Intelligence." In *Encyclopedia of Applied Psychology,* ed. C. Speilberger. San Diego, Calif.: Academic Press.

Chopra, D. (1991). "What Is the True Nature of Reality? The Basics of Quantum Healing." Talk given at the Seattle Center on May 18, 1991. Available at http://www.ascension-research.org/reality.html.

Cohen, A. (2005, Jan. 28). "Denver Law Firm's Demise a Lesson for Us All." *Denver Post,* p. 7B.

Collins, J. (2001). *Good to Great.* New York: HarperCollins.

Cousins, N. (1964). *Anatomy of an Illness as Perceived by the Patient: Reflections on Healing and Regeneration.* New York: Norton.

Dalai Lama and Cutler, H. C. (1998). *The Art of Happiness: A Handbook for Living.* New York: Riverhead Books.

Druskat, V. U., and Wolff, S. B. (2001, Mar.). "Building the Emotional Intelligence of Groups." *Harvard Business Review,* pp. 81–90.

Eisenberger, N., Lieberman, M. D., and Williams, K. D. (2003, Oct. 10). "Does Rejection Hurt? An FMRI Study of Social Exclusion." *Science,* 302: 290–292.

Elfenbein, H. A. (2006). "Team Emotional Intelligence: What It Can Mean and How It Can Affect Performance." In *Linking Emotional Intelligence and Performance at Work: Current Research Evidence with Individuals and Groups,* ed. V. U. Druskat, F. Sala, and G. Mount. Mahwah, N.J.: Erlbaum.

Emmerling, R. J., and Goleman, D. (2003). "Emotional Intelligence: Issues and Common Misunderstandings." Available at www.eiconsortium. org/research/EI_Issues_And_Common_Misunderstandings.pdf.

Fisher, R., and Ury, W. (1981). *Getting to Yes: Negotiating Agreement Without Giving In,* ed. B. Patton. Boston: Houghton Mifflin.

Friedman, T. (1999). *The Lexus and the Olive Tree.* New York: Anchor Books.

Gibson, D., and Tulgan, B. (2002). *Managing Anger in the Workplace.* Amherst, Mass.: HRD Press.

Gladwell, M. (2005). *Blink.* New York: Little, Brown.

Golden, J., Rice, R., and Yant Kinney, M. (2002). *Philadelphia Murals.* Philadelphia: Temple University Press.

Goleman, D. (2006). *Social Intelligence.* New York: Bantam.

Hanh, T. N. (2001). *Anger.* New York: Riverhead Books.

Harvey, A. (1995). "Introduction." In Dalai Lama, *Essential Teachings.* North Atlantic Books.

Hobson, A. J. (2000). *Consciousness.* New York: Scientific American Library.

Hughes, M. (2006). *Life's 2% Solution*. Boston: NicholasBrealey.

Hughes, M., Patterson, L. B., and Terrell, J. B. (2005). *Emotional Intelligence in Action: Training and Coaching Activities for Leaders and Managers*. San Francisco: Jossey-Bass/Pfeiffer.

Hunter, J. E., Schmidt, F. D., and Judiesch, M. K. (1990). "Individual Differences in Output Variability as a Function of Job Complexity." *Journal of Applied Psychology*, 75: 28–42.

Hurley, R. (2006, Sept.). "The Decision to Trust." *Harvard Business Review*, pp. 55–62.

Huseman, R. C., and Hatfield, J. D. (1989). *Managing the Equity Factor*. Boston: Houghton Mifflin.

James, J. (1996). *Thinking in the Future Tense*. New York: Simon & Schuster.

Jones, D. (2006, June 7). "Not All Successful CEOs Are Extroverts." *USA Today*, pp. 1B–2B.

Jordan, P., and Ashkanasy, N. M. (2006). "Emotional Intelligence, Emotional Self-Awareness, and Team Effectiveness." In *Linking Emotional Intelligence and Performance at Work: Current Research Evidence with Individuals and Groups*, ed. V. U. Druskat, F. Sala, and G. Mount. Mahwah, N.J.: Erlbaum.

LeDoux, J. E. (1996). *The Emotional Brain: The Mysterious Underpinnings of Emotional Life*. New York: Simon & Schuster.

Lencioni, P. (2002). *The Five Dysfunctions of a Team*. San Francisco: Jossey-Bass.

Mackey, J. (2006, Nov. 2). "Compensation at Whole Foods Market." http://www.wholefoods.com/blogs/jm/archives/2006/11/compensation_at_1.html.

Maslow, A. H. (1943). "A Theory of Human Motivation." *Psychological Review*, 50: 370–396.

McClelland, D. C. (1999). "Identifying Competencies with Behavioral-Event Interviews." *Psychological Science*, 9: 331–339. Available at http://www.eiconsortium.org/research/business_case_for_ei.htm.

Offermann, L. R., Bailey, J. R., Vasilopoulos, N. L., Seal, C., and Sass, M. (2004). "The Relative Contribution of Emotional Competence and Cognitive Ability to Individual and Team Performance." *Human Performance*, 17: 219–243.

Pearson, C. M., Anderson, L. M., and Porath, C. L. (2000). "Assessing and Attacking Workplace Incivility." *Organizational Dynamics*, 29: 123–137.

Pert, C. (1997). *The Molecules of Emotion*. New York: Simon & Schuster.

Pert, C. (2004). *Your Body Is Your Subconscious Mind*. Boulder, Colo.: Sounds True.

Pink, D. (2005). *A Whole New Mind*. New York: Riverhead Books.

Plutchik, R. (2001). "The Nature of Emotions." *American Scientist,* 89: 344–345.

Rath, T. (2006). *Vital Friends: The People You Can't Live Without.* New York: Gallup Press.

Ray, P., and Anderson, S. R. (2000). *The Cultural Creatives.* New York: Harmony Books.

Reber, A. (1985). *The Dictionary of Psychology.* New York: Penguin.

Rock, D., and Schwartz, J. (2006, Summer). "The Neuroscience of Leadership." *Strategy and Business.* Available at http://www.strategy-business.com/press/freearticle/06207.

Row, H. (1998, Nov.). "Coping—Martin Seligman." *Fast Company,* p. 196.

Ruderman, M. N., Hannum, K., Leslie, J. B., and Steed, J. (2001). *Leadership Skills and Emotional Intelligence.* Colorado Springs, Colo.: Center for Creative Leadership.

Russell, P. (1992). *Waking Up in Time.* Novato, Calif.: Origin Press.

Salovey, P., and Mayer, J. D. (1990). "Emotional Intelligence." *Imagination, Cognition, and Personality,* 9: 185–211.

Secretary's Commission on Achieving Necessary Skills (SCANS). (1991, June). *What Work Requires of Schools: A SCANS Report for America 2000.* Washington, D.C.: U.S. Department of Labor.

Seligman, M.E.P. (1991). *Learned Optimism.* New York: Knopf.

Seligman, M.E.P. (2002). *Authentic Happiness.* New York: Free Press.

Seyle, H. (1974). *Stress Without Distress.* Philadelphia: Lippincott.

Spencer, L. M. (2001). "The Economic Value of Emotional Intelligence Competencies and EIC-Based HR Programs." In *The Emotionally Intelligent Workplace,* ed. C. Cherniss and D. Goleman. San Francisco: Jossey-Bass.

Stein, S. J. (2007). *Make Your Workplace Great: The Seven Keys to an Emotionally Intelligent Organization.* San Francisco: Jossey-Bass/Pfeiffer.

Stein, S. J., and Book, H. E. (2000). *The EQ Edge: Emotional Intelligence and Your Success.* Toronto: Multi-Health Systems.

Sweetman, K. (2001, Fall). "Don't Worry, Be Happy." *MIT Sloan Management Review,* p. 10.

Thorndike, E. L. (1920). "Intelligence and Its Uses." *Harper Magazine,* 140: 227–235.

Tuckman, B. W. (1965). "Developmental Sequence in Small Groups." *Psychological Bulletin,* 63: 384–399.

Tuckman, B. W., and Jensen, M.A.C. (1977). "Stages of Small Group Development Revisited." *Group and Organizational Studies,* 2: 419–427.

Warren, R. (2002). *The Purpose Driven Life.* Grand Rapids, Mich.: Zondervan.

Wheeler, S. (2004, Sept. 22). "Taking 'Helping the Homeless' to Extremes." *Denver Post,* pp. 1F, 10F.

Wolff, S. A., Druskat, V. U., Koman, E. S., and Messer, T. E. (2006). "The Link Between Group Emotional Competence and Group Effectiveness." In *Linking Emotional Intelligence and Performance at Work: Current Research Evidence with Individuals and Groups,* ed. V. U. Druskat, F. Sala, and G. Mount. Mahwah, N.J.: Erlbaum.

ACKNOWLEDGMENTS

The authors wish to acknowledge and thank all of the following people:

The many teams and organizations that we have had the great honor to work with. You teach us daily.

Steven Stein, David Groth, Diana Durek, and all our brilliant colleagues at Multi-Health Systems who promote emotional intelligence daily. Reuven Bar-On, Peter Salovey, John D. Mayer, David R. Caruso, Daniel Goleman, Cary Cherniss, Richard E. Boyatzis, and Annie McKee for your pioneering emotional intelligence work.

Neal Mallett, editor at Jossey-Bass, for welcoming, guiding, and masterfully bringing this book to reality together with the Jossey-Bass team; Martin Delahoussaye, senior editor at Pfeiffer, for guiding and encouraging us with such good cheer; Mark Karmendy, editorial production manager; Bruce Emmer, copyeditor; Sarah Miller, cleanup editor; Carolyn Miller Carlstroem, senior marketing manager; Amie Wong, marketing assistant; and Rob Brandt, editorial projects manager, for help with global rights licensing.

Michael Snell, our agent, for creating an excellent interface with our publisher and orchestrating a win-win process and continuing down the publishing path with us.

Carina Fiedeldey-Van Dijk, of ePsy Consultancy, for assistance in clarifying our Team Emotional and Social Intelligence Survey; O C O'Connell for being with us through thick and thin, insisting on quality, getting us to laugh along the way, and for her much-needed editing assistance; and Beverly Swanson for help with document preparation and graphic design.

Robert Carkhuff, John Grinder, Richard Bandler, Leslie Lebeau, Judith DeLozier, and Robert Dilts and all their teachers for the phenomenal contributions they have made to our understanding of human communication and how to improve it.

James would like to acknowledge his high school teacher Ken Mowery as an incorrigible coadventurer on our preposterous planet and thank him for over thirty-five years of mentorship, teaching, and friendship. (I draw on it every day.)

Our daughter, Julia, who smiled, encouraged us, and demonstrated infinite patience with long hours and late dinners. Our brother, Don Hughes, and all of our parents, families, friends, teachers, mentors, clients, and adversaries, and the grace and pluck that have gotten us each this far along the crazy paths we call our lives.

ABOUT THE AUTHORS

Marcia Hughes is president of Collaborative Growth LLC and serves as a strategic communications partner for leaders and teams in organizations that value high performers. She weaves her expertise in emotional intelligence throughout her consulting work, facilitation, team building, and workshops to help people motivate themselves and communicate more effectively with others. Her keynotes are built around powerful stories of how success can grow when people work collaboratively. Businesses, government agencies, and nonprofits have all benefited in such areas as team and leadership development, strategic design, and conflict resolution from her proven formula for success. She is coauthor of *Emotional Intelligence in Action* and author of *Life's 2% Solution*.

Hughes is a certified trainer in the Bar-On EQ-i and EQ 360. She certifies senior human resource leaders, coaches, and consultants to use these measures with the people they lead. She provides Train the Trainer training and coaching in powerful EQ delivery. Her inspiration and persistent efforts led the development, promotion, and hosting of Collaborative Growth's International EQ Symposium in 2004 and attracted participants from nine nations. It focused on distilling effective strategies for behavioral change from the theory and research on emotional intelligence.

Her efforts to improve productivity in the workplace through strategic communication grew out of a distinguished career in law where her firm specialized in complex public policy matters. There again her leadership and communication skills enabled Hughes's team to effectively address controversial environmental, land use, and water development matters involving numerous stakeholders, which included federal, state, and local governments along with the general public.

As an assistant attorney general, she served the Department of Public Health and the Environment; additionally, she clerked on the 10th Circuit Court of Appeals for the Honorable William E. Doyle and served with the Environmental Protection Agency in Washington, D.C.

James Bradford Terrell is vice president of Collaborative Growth LLC, where he applies his expertise in interpersonal communication to help a variety of public and private sector clients anticipate change and respond to it resiliently.

Coauthor of *Emotional Intelligence in Action,* he coaches leaders, teams in transition, and senior management using the Bar-On EQ-i, the EQ 360, and other measures. He also works as a contract mediator for the U.S. Forest Service and other federal agencies.

Terrell was instrumental in developing, promoting, and hosting Collaborative Growth's International EQ Symposium in 2004 and is leading the development of future symposiums. He provides Train the Trainer workshops and teaches other coaches how to develop insightful interpretations and creative applications of EQ results.

He worked as a psychotherapist in private practice for many years, seeing primarily clients whose general goal was to resolve conflict in relationships—with spouses, children, parents, employers, and coworkers. For three years, he served as executive director of the Syntropy Institute, a not-for-profit research organization investigating how communication training influences human effectiveness. He also served as the director of training for the Metro-Denver Mutual Housing Association, an early developer of cooperative housing in the Denver area.

In an earlier life, he was the owner and operator of Integrity Building Systems, a construction company specializing in residential and commercial renovation, and served as a project coordinator on a wide variety of building projects including Denver International Airport and the National Digital Cable Television Center. In a future life, he is certain he will be a rock star.

INDEX

Page numbers in italics refer to figures, exhibits, and tables.